Reading through Romans

READING THROUGH
ROMANS

C. K. BARRETT

FORTRESS PRESS
Philadelphia

First American Edition by Fortress Press 1977

© 1977 by SCM Press Limited, London
and Fortress Press, Philadelphia

Library of Congress Catalog Card Number 76-55828

ISBN 0-8006-1250-7

Printed in Great Britain   1-1250

CONTENTS

	Preface	vii
1	The Gospel	1
2	The Wrath of God	5
3	All have Sinned	10
4	God's Righteousness	14
5	Faith	18
6	Justification	22
7	So Wide...	26
8	The New Life	30
9	What is Religion?	34
10	Life in the Spirit	38
11	If God is For Us ...	41
12	The People of God	46
13	Christ the End of the Law	51
14	The Way God Works	55
15	Mercy Triumphant	59
16	Life in the Church	64
17	Perfect Love	68
18	How to Deal with a Problem	72
19	An Evangelist and his Plans	77
20	Products of the Gospel	82

PREFACE

The twenty studies in this little book have long been out of print, and I am grateful to the SCM Press for the suggestion that they might be re-issued. I hope they may give some help to those who are feeling their way into the regular use of the Bible. It will be wise always to read the relevant section of Romans first, then the three or four pages of comment, and finally the text of Romans once more. The text given for convenience at the head of each section is that of the Revised Standard Version, but any of the current translations could be used, and the reader will often gain a great deal through comparing them. It will be clear even to the most uninstructed that I have not attempted anything like a complete and systematic exposition of the epistle, or to set out its message in a new idiom – such restatements are not always an improvement on the original. In general I have avoided the more difficult and obscure passages, and concentrated on those where I felt reasonably confident that I could convey something of Paul's meaning to a reader with no technical equipment – though I have always assumed a serious desire to hear and understand God's word. Given such a desire, there is much in Romans that speaks directly to anyone who will listen, and speaks of Christian fundamentals that are too often by-passed today. Those who wish to go further will find more in my commentary on Romans published (in 1957, and often reprinted) by A. & C. Black in the series *Black's New Testament Commentaries*, and more still in the fuller and more detailed commentary by my friend and colleague C. E. B. Cranfield, published by T. & C. Clark in 1975 in the *International Critical Commentary* series.

These studies were first published at fortnightly intervals in the journal *Advance*, edited by Amos Cresswell, who gave permission for republication by the Epworth Press in 1963. I do not apologize for the fact that, even after some revision, they still bear some traces of this Methodist origin. The Wesleys knew what Romans was about, and there are worse guides.

Durham   C. K. BARRETT
August 1976

The Gospel

1 Paul, a servant of Jesus Christ, called to be an apostle, set apart for the gospel of God ²which he promised beforehand through his prophets in the holy scriptures, ³the gospel concerning his Son, who was descended from David according to the flesh ⁴and designated Son of God in power according to the Spirit of holiness by his resurrection from the dead, Jesus Christ our Lord, ⁵through whom we have received grace and apostleship to bring about the obedience of faith for the sake of his name among all the nations, ⁶including yourselves who are called to belong to Jesus Christ;

7 To all God's beloved in Rome, who are called to be saints:

Grace to you and peace from God our Father and the Lord Jesus Christ.

8 First, I thank my God through Jesus Christ for all of you, because your faith is proclaimed in all the world. ⁹For God is my witness, whom I serve with my spirit in the gospel of his Son, that without ceasing I mention you always in my prayers, ¹⁰asking that somehow by God's will I may now at last succeed in coming to you. ¹¹For I long to see you, that I may impart to you some spiritual gift to strengthen you, ¹²that is, that we may be mutually encouraged by each other's faith, both yours and mine. ¹³I want you to know, brethren, that I have often intended to come to you (but thus far have been prevented), in order that I may reap some harvest among you as well as among the rest of the Gentiles. ¹⁴I am under obligation both to Greeks and to barbarians, both to the wise and to the foolish: ¹⁵so I am eager to preach the gospel to you also who are in Rome.

16 For I am not ashamed of the gospel: it is the power of God for salvation to every one who has faith, to the Jew first and also to the Greek. ¹⁷For in it the righteousness of God is revealed through faith for faith; as it is written, 'He who through faith is righteous shall live.'

Many people have the impression that Paul's letters are difficult to understand, and that Romans is perhaps the hardest of them all. It is certainly true that no book that deals responsibly with the deepest issues of life and death, of God and man, can be glanced through like a strip cartoon. Yet Luther could call Romans 'the plainest gospel of all', and we can be sure that Paul himself wrote it not for a few picked theologians but for all the Christians in Rome. And it is still true that anyone who reads it as seriously as Paul wrote it, and with the same dependence on the Spirit of truth, can get at the heart of the matter.

Paul was a practical missionary; he was planning a journey to Spain (15.24, 28), for which his old bases (Antioch and Ephesus) would have been comparatively useless, and he had therefore to introduce himself and his message to the capital of the West. There was a church there, but he had not founded it. He could not ask its support without presenting his credentials, and his credentials were – the gospel. He had no other (Galatians 1.8).

In this opening section there are two paragraphs into which Paul packs much of what he understood by the gospel. The first paragraph is the address (1.1–7), which has the usual form taken by a letter in Paul's day, except that the names of both the sender (Paul), and the recipients (God's beloved in Rome) are expanded by Christian definitions, and the greeting becomes a Christian prayer (grace and peace). Paul in these opening verses brings out the fact that the gospel is about God's Son, Jesus Christ. It is not a religious philosophy, a religious experience, or a religious society. It is the record of the great things God has done for men in Christ. God had first of all made his plans known through the prophets in the Old Testament, which is thus essentially a Christian book – Christian because its central theme is Christ, 'the Christ who was to come'. Throughout the letter Paul's argument will again and again remind us that no Christian can dispense with the Old Testament, not because the Old Testament is an interesting source

2

for the history of religions, but because it points to Christ. The central point, however, is that what God had long ago foretold he has now fulfilled. Two things have to be said about Jesus Christ, in whom the fulfilment happened. On the one hand, he was a man, a Jew, a descendant of David. We shall see later how Paul insists that Jesus shared our nature to the full (see 8.3). On the other hand, he was God's Son; and what this means is seen in an event that has happened to no one else in all history – the resurrection of the dead. Jesus is all that we are, and all that we are not; in him God himself acted in such a way that our world could never be the same again.

Because Jesus was what he was, we Christians are what we are. Because he is the Lord, we are his slaves, owing him total obedience. Because he is holy, we are called to be saints, that is, the holy people of God, marked out for his own possession. Because he is God's Son, there is a gospel, and some men, like Paul, are set apart for the task of proclaiming it.

The second paragraph in which Paul sums up the gospel is 1.16, 17. Paul will preach it anywhere, even in Rome. Nothing need, or can, shame him into silence. In the gospel, he says, there is revealed God's righteousness. This is a very important word, and we shall understand it fully only as we go on to study the way in which Paul uses it in various parts of the letter. At the core of the idea is something God does. Certainly he is righteous; he also does the right, and for him doing the right means putting things and people right. For this reason the word righteousness is closely connected in the Bible with salvation (as it is at 1.16, 17; also, for example, in Isaiah 51.5, 6; see RV). Because God himself is right he makes rightness possible for men. There is more in God's righteousness than this, as we shall see; but this is the essential point here. God's righteousness puts men right, and this – this alone – makes available a power leading to salvation. All that man can contribute to the process is the faith in which he takes God at his word, and lets him do his righteous work. Faith, and nothing but faith: what this means too we have still to learn.

3

But Paul knows what it is to live by faith (Habakkuk 2.4); and out of this knowledge comes the way in which he deals with the practical issues of life: his zeal for spreading the gospel (1.9, 10, 13–15), his joy in the faith of his fellow-Christians (1.8), his prayers (1.9, 10), and his modesty and humility (1.12).

2 | 1.18–2.16

The Wrath of God

18 For the wrath of God is revealed from heaven against all ungodliness and wickedness of men who by their wickedness suppress the truth. ¹⁹For what can be known about God is plain to them, because God has shown it to them. ²⁰Ever since the creation of the world his invisible nature, namely, his eternal power and deity, has been clearly perceived in the things that have been made. So they are without excuse; ²¹for although they knew God they did not honour him as God or give thanks to him, but they became futile in their thinking and their senseless minds were darkened. ²²Claiming to be wise, they became fools, ²³and exchanged the glory of the immortal God for images resembling mortal man or birds or animals or reptiles.

24 Therefore God gave them up in the lusts of their hearts to impurity, to the dishonouring of their bodies among themselves, ²⁵because they exchanged the truth about God for a lie and worshipped and served the creature rather than the Creator, who is blessed for ever! Amen.

26 For this reason God gave them up to dishonourable passions. Their women exchanged natural relations for unnatural, ²⁷and the men likewise gave up natural relations with women and were consumed with passion for one another, men committing shameless acts with men and receiving in their own persons the due penalty for their error.

28 And since they did not see fit to acknowledge God, God gave them up to a base mind and to improper conduct. ²⁹They were filled with all manner of wickedness, evil, covetousness, malice. Full of envy, murder, strife, deceit, malignity, they are gossips, ³⁰slanderers, haters of God, insolent, haughty, boastful, inventors of evil, disobedient to parents, ³¹foolish, faithless, heartless, ruthless. ³²Though they know God's decree that those who do such things deserve to die, they not only do them but approve those who practise them.

2 Therefore you have no excuse, O man, whoever you are, when you judge another; for in passing judgment upon him you condemn yourself, because you, the judge, are doing the very same things.

5

²We know that the judgment of God rightly falls upon those who do such things. ³Do you suppose, O man, that when you judge those who do such things and yet do them yourself, you will escape the judgment of God? ⁴Or do you presume upon the riches of his kindness and forbearance and patience? Do you not know that God's kindness is meant to lead you to repentance? ⁵But by your hard and impenitent heart you are storing up wrath for yourself on the day of wrath when God's righteous judgment will be revealed. ⁶For he will render to every man according to his works: ⁷to those who by patience in well-doing seek for glory and honour and immortality, he will give eternal life; ⁸but for those who are factious and do not obey the truth, but obey wickedness, there will be wrath and fury. ⁹There will be tribulation and distress for every human being who does evil, the Jew first and also the Greek, ¹⁰but glory and honour and peace for every one who does good, the Jew first and also the Greek. ¹¹For God shows no partiality.

12 All who have sinned without the law will also perish without the law, and all who have sinned under the law will be judged by the law. ¹³For it is not the hearers of the law who are righteous before God, but the doers of the law who will be justified. ¹⁴When Gentiles who have not the law do by nature what the law requires, they are a law to themselves, even though they do not have the law. ¹⁵They show that what the law requires is written on their hearts, while their conscience also bears witness and their conflicting thoughts accuse or perhaps excuse them ¹⁶on that day when, according to my gospel, God judges the secrets of men by Christ Jesus.

In the opening paragraphs of his letter, Paul states what the gospel is – the revealing of God's righteousness (1.17), his activity in putting things and people right. But what Paul has said about the gospel as a divine power leading to salvation (1.16) presupposes a certain amount of readiness to be put right; a recognition that things are wrong and that only God can mend them. This is part of the meaning of faith, which also means laying hold on Christ and his promises. But suppose this faith is absent; does this mean that God will be shut out of his world, and unable to act within it? No; but it does mean that his activity will take a different and terrible form.

To this form of God's activity, the opposite of salvation, Paul gives the name *wrath* (1.18; 2.5, 8); and what he describes in

1.21 is the opposite of faith: when men are faced with God they refuse to treat him as God, that is, to glorify him and give thanks to him. (Note that faith means that we let God be the sort of God he wishes to be, and give thanks to him for his goodness.) Men refuse to treat God as God, because to do so means recognizing someone who is *the Lord*, someone who stands outside ourselves as the author of our life, and has the right to claim our obedience. No one can recognize this Lord and at the same time retain his independence; so, because man wishes to be both independent and 'religious', he manufactures other gods (1.23), whom he has no need to fear and obey.

I said, 'when men are faced with God'. But are they? Paul must have known that only a minute fraction of the world's population had heard the gospel; he cannot be thinking of those who had heard it and rejected it. In fact, what he says is based upon the story of Adam, which reflects the experience of the human race as a whole. He does not teach that man can look round the world and from it prove the existence of the God whom we know in Jesus Christ; he teaches exactly the opposite. Man lives in a world where the very existence of things that he has not himself made should teach him that there is a God to honour and obey; but such is his nature that he prefers to be his own god, and to pass by the Creator. This is in some ways the most difficult thought to grasp in the whole letter, but it is essential to understand it, or Paul's gospel will not shine out in the clearest light. We shall see in a moment that this turning from God may result in sheer moral wickedness or in priggish respectability; *in either case* we have to do with what Luther called 'the heart turned in upon itself', the heart that enthrones itself in God's place.

Whenever this happens, God's wrath is inevitably, if secretly, at work. Men lose the knowledge of God they should have had, and the more they make themselves out to be wise the more foolish they become (1.22). Moreover, even when they know (1.32) God's sentence on sin, they plunge into it, and Paul gives a horrifying list of the things men can do (1.28–31). Study the list, and see what happens when a man dethrones God and puts himself at the centre of his own life; he fails to recognize his obligations to others, and exploits their property and even their bodies to serve his desire.

So much for chapter 1; Paul paints a dark picture, but no one who knows the ancient world can doubt that parts of it at least were as dark as the picture. There were, however, other parts. There were critics of the downward trend in morals, both Gentile philosophers and Jewish teachers (the latter are in mind here, as 2.9, 10 show, but receive fuller treatment from 2.17 onwards). Here, surely, one might say, are men who will escape Paul's censure and God's judgment. By no means. The clue to chapter 2 is in the first verse: 'you are doing the very same things'. This does not mean that all the moral critics were actually guilty of all the sins described in 1.28–31; this would simply not be true. It means that by setting themselves up as judges they too are putting themselves in God's place, since it is God's business to judge the world (3.6). Indeed, he will judge; he will judge *all* men, without respect of persons (2.11), and he will judge not by outward appearance but by the secret things of the heart (2.16). Two further points are made about the judgment in verses 7 and 8. The way that leads to eternal life is marked by patience in well-doing. What this suggests is shown by 8.25; it means not only perseverance but a willingness to look in hope beyond our activity to what God will do. The way that leads to wrath and anger is marked by a servile spirit, out to make profit for itself by means of its behaviour. God will not be deceived by it; nor, in the end, will our own conscience (2.15).

I repeat: this is a difficult passage; many of the details there is no space to explain here. The main points to grasp are these:

1. Man is God's creature, and it is for him to recognize his Creator as his Lord, to love, honour, and trust him.

2. Man's fundamental fault is to put himself in God's place.

3. This issues sometimes in immoral life, sometimes in arrogant religiosity – both equally blameworthy.

4. Man's own conscience accuses him, and the only way (hinted at here, developed later) to escape the wrath with which God visits sin is the way of hope and faith.

2.17–3.20

All have Sinned

17 But if you call yourself a Jew and rely upon the law and boast of your relation to God ¹⁸ and know his will and approve what is excellent, because you are instructed in the law, ¹⁹ and if you are sure that you are a guide to the blind, a light to those who are in darkness, ²⁰ a corrector of the foolish, a teacher of children, having in the law the embodiment of knowledge and truth – ²¹ you then who teach others, will you not teach yourself? While you preach against stealing, do you steal? ²² You who say that one must not commit adultery, do you commit adultery? You who abhor idols, do you rob temples? ²³ You who boast in the law, do you dishonour God by breaking the law? ²⁴ For, as it is written, 'The name of God is blasphemed among the Gentiles because of you.'

25 Circumcision indeed is of value if you obey the law; but if you break the law, your circumcision becomes uncircumcision. ²⁶ So, if a man who is uncircumcised keeps the precepts of the law, will not his uncircumcision be regarded as circumcision? ²⁷ Then those who are physically uncircumcised but keep the law will condemn you who have the written code and circumcision but break the law. ²⁸ For he is not a real Jew who is one outwardly, nor is true circumcision something external and physical. ²⁹ He is a Jew who is one inwardly, and real circumcision is a matter of the heart, spiritual and not literal. His praise is not from men but from God.

3 Then what advantage has the Jew? Or what is the value of circumcision? ²ᴹuch in every way. To begin with, the Jews are entrusted with the oracles of God. ³ What if some were unfaithful? Does their faithlessness nullify the faithfulness of God? ⁴ By no means! Let God be true though every man be false, as it is written,

'That thou mayest be justified in thy words,
and prevail when thou art judged.'

⁵ But if our wickedness serves to show the justice of God, what shall we say? That God is unjust to inflict wrath on us? (I speak in a human way.) ⁶ By no means! For then how could God judge the world? ⁷ But if through my falsehood God's truthfulness abounds to

his glory, why am I still being condemned as a sinner? [8] And why not do evil that good may come? – as some people slanderously charge us with saying. Their condemnation is just.

9 What then? Are we Jews any better off? No, not at all; for I have already charged that all men, both Jews and Greeks, are under the power of sin, [10] as it is written:

'None is righteous, no, not one;
[11] no one understands, no one seeks for God.
[12] All have turned aside, together they have gone wrong;
no one does good, not even one.'
[13] 'Their throat is an open grave,
they use their tongues to deceive.'
'The venom of asps is under their lips.'
[14] 'Their mouth is full of curses and bitterness.'
[15] 'Their feet are swift to shed blood,
[16] in their paths are ruin and misery,
[17] and the way of peace they do not know.'
[18] 'There is no fear of God before their eyes.'

19 Now we know that whatever the law says it speaks to those who are under the law, so that every mouth may be stopped, and the whole world may be held accountable to God. [20] For no human being will be justified in his sight by works of the law, since through the law comes knowledge of sin.

We have now followed Paul through a clear-sighted and profound analysis not simply of the world of his own time, but of human nature as it always is – an analysis so profound that it takes hard thinking to trace it out. Yet the drift is clear: there are some (1.21–31) who have simply turned their backs on God and sunk into the depths of wickedness; there are others who would do the same if they dared, but in fact only 'approve' what is done (1.32); and there are others again who stand in the pulpit of moral and spiritual pride to condemn their fellows (2.1–11). All come under condemnation, for all are doing the same thing; all are depriving God of his due by putting themselves in his place.

There is, however, one class of men who can claim a special right to set themselves up as judges – the Jews. There is the man (2.17–20) who bears the name of 'Jew', who rests upon the law, who glories in God, and knows his will, and approves the things that are excellent, being instructed out of the law, confident that he is a guide of the blind, a light of those that are in darkness, having in the law the very embodiment of knowledge and of the truth. Here is someone whose judgment must surely be valid. There is something in this claim, at least to the extent that the law itself (the Old Testament) is spiritual (7.14), and that to possess it is the greatest of privileges (3.2); but this is not the question here. The question is not about the truth of God's word, but the standing of the man who passes judgment on others. And here the principle of 2.1 applies again: You, who judge, do the same things as the man you condemn (2.21–24). These verses do not mean that all Jews are guilty of theft, adultery, and sacrilege in the ordinary sense of the words. Paul is giving the words the same sort of interpretation that Jesus gave in the Sermon on the Mount (see Matthew 5.21–48). Understand these crimes in their deepest sense, and there is no man who is not guilty of them. The mere fact of being a Jew, the mere fact of having the Old Testament in his hands, does not mean that any man can at the same time judge his fellows and escape judgment himself.

The key to the last paragraph in chapter 2 (verses 25–29) is given in verses 25 and 26. Circumcision, Paul says, is a good thing – *if you do the law*. But a Jew would reply: This is non-sense. Circumcision is part of the law, and you cannot possibly keep the precepts of the law (2.26) if you are not circumcised. It is clear that by 'keeping the precepts of the law' Paul must mean something different from the simple observance of par-ticular commandments. As we shall see later, the law, though open to perversion and abuse (7.8, 11, 13), is nevertheless a good and holy gift from God to men (7.12); it points to the true relation between God and man, though it lacks the power to achieve it (8.3). When rightly understood, it teaches that man should live in humble believing dependence on God. This, not the keeping of rules such as circumcision, is the essential thing. It follows that a man may be circumcised – and not truly keep the law; his circumcision then becomes worthless. It also follows that an uncircumcised man may observe the essence of the law; his uncircumcision does not count against him. The circumcision that matters is circumcision of the heart (2.29; compare Deuteronomy 30.6; Jeremiah 4.4).

But now Paul has landed himself in a series of difficulties. If all this is true, what is the good of being a Jew (3.1)? This is a serious question, because it was God who called and made the Jewish people, and if there is no good in being a Jew it means that God's work has come to nothing. But the Jew has an advantage. He has the Bible (the oracles of God, 3.2). To him as to no one else, God's truth and God's command have been made known. This is indeed a privilege, but a very terrible one (compare Amos 3.2). After showing (in 3.10–18) the Bible's own accusation of sinful man, Paul sums up in 3.19, 20. The law speaks to the Jews as representatives of the whole world. If they are guilty, all are guilty. No one, of any nation or age, can ever put himself right with God by his own actions. It is a bleak prospect; but the last word has not been spoken yet.

Looking back, there are two chief things to learn.

1. The unity of the Bible. Paul is above all things a preacher of the gospel, but he uses the Old Testament, and uses it not only in condemnation but also as a book that bears witness to God's love and to the way of faith. All this will come out more clearly later, but it is implied in chapters 2 and 3.

2. It must have cost Paul a good deal to write about the Jews as he did; he was no anti-Semite. He sees in his own people the clearest picture of religion – man's way of climbing up to God by means of his own piety and virtue. And this way, he says, will not work. Our own piety, our own good deeds, our own churchmanship; all in the end count for nothing. '*Nothing* in my hand I bring.'

4

God's Righteousness

21 But now the righteousness of God has been manifested apart from law, although the law and the prophets bear witness to it, ²² the righteousness of God through faith in Jesus Christ for all who believe. For there is no distinction; ²³ since all have sinned and fall short of the glory of God, ²⁴ they are justified by his grace as a gift, through the redemption which is in Christ Jesus, ²⁵ whom God put forward as an expiation by his blood, to be received by faith. This was to show God's righteousness, because in his divine forbearance he had passed over former sins; ²⁶ it was to prove at the present time that he himself is righteous and that he justifies him who has faith in Jesus.

27 Then what becomes of our boasting? It is excluded. On what principle? On the principle of works? No, but on the principle of faith. ²⁸ For we hold that a man is justified by faith apart from works of law. ²⁹ Or is God the God of Jews only? Is he not the God of Gentiles also? Yes, of Gentiles also, ³⁰ since God is one; and he will justify the circumcised on the ground of their faith and the uncircumcised through their faith. ³¹ Do we then overthrow the law by this faith? By no means! On the contrary, we uphold the law.

It is not a good thing to try to write Paul's letters for him. He could do it quite well for himself. All the same, it may not be wrong at this stage to pause before reading the next paragraph of Romans, and ask what Paul is likely to do next. Is there anything he can do? He has shown us a picture of men who by conventional standards are 'bad' men, and of others who are 'good'. Both fall under God's judgment; there is not, in God's eyes, a single righteous man among them (3.10). It is not that they have had no chance. All should have perceived God's 'eternal power and deity' (1.20), but, though set in a world full of his glory, they have passed by unheeding.

More, to some of those involved God had spoken his own word in the law (the Old Testament: 2.18; 3.2); even so, they had not listened, or rather had twisted God's word into a legalistic religion God never intended. What in these circumstances can even an apostle say? What can even God do?

We know the answer, though we know it only because we have 'cheated' – we have looked ahead, and know what Paul says in the next paragraph. The answer is, that God must manifest his righteousness in a new way, that does at least these two things. (1) It must reveal more of him than his power, and the way he is to be obeyed – it must reveal his love. (2) It must be incapable of being perverted by man's self-centredness. These points, and much more beside, we shall find in 3.21–31, perhaps the richest and most important paragraph in the whole letter.

God has revealed his righteousness apart from the law, though, since God is always the same God, if you read the Old Testament with Christian eyes you can find there a witness to the gospel (3.21). Law, however good, can always be twisted; in God's new act of revelation this danger does not exist, because it is received not by obedience to rule, but through faith in Jesus Christ (3.22), and faith means man's recognition that there is nothing he can do to save himself, and that he must simply put his trust in God's mercy. God revealed his righteousness by revealing his love, his mercy, the grace by which men are freely justified (3.24). But there is a good deal here that calls for explanation.

'Justification' calls up a picture of God's court, in which guilty man is arraigned before his judge. What will happen to him? Surely he will be condemned and punished. What else can he expect? Certainly God cannot, and does not, say that the sinner, even though penitent and believing, is after all good. This would be a lie, and God does not lie. But God does say, 'You, who have been my enemy, are now going to be my friend. Things have been wrong between us; now they are going to be right.' This is what justification means – the righting of relations between God and man. It is something man can never do for himself; but God can do it, and does. Even God, however, does not do it easily. He does it only by 'the redemption which is in Christ Jesus'. To Paul's readers, 'redemption' would suggest the freeing of a slave by the payment of a price; and this time God paid the price.

There is more to say about this, and Paul says it in 3.25. God redeemed men when he set forth his son Jesus Christ as a *propitiation*. This is the word used in the AV, but it does not give us the whole truth. The RSV, by using the word *expiation*, gives us another part of Paul's meaning at the expense of the first. 'Propitiation' is not adequate, for this means that the offender does something to appease the person he has offended, whereas Paul says that God himself 'put forward' Christ. Propitiation is truly there, however, for, through the sacrifice of Christ, God's wrath is turned away; but behind the propitiation lies the fact that God has actually wiped out (*expiated*) our sin, and made us right with himself. Paul's word also suggests the lid of the ark, where the Jewish high priest sprinkled the blood that made atonement for his people (Leviticus 16).

One step more will bring us through the argument. Notice how Paul fastens on the *present* time (3.26). What God does now in Christ makes sense of both the past (when God might seem to have passed over sin without caring), and the future (in which we face God's judgment without fear because he has already forgiven us). God is shown to be righteous, because the cross shows his hatred of sin, and in his saving righteousness he justifies the man who accepts Christ crucified and risen as the supreme sign of his love (5.8).

We are through the argument; and the thanksgiving can begin. If Paul has used a certain amount of theological language he has done so not in order to obscure but to safeguard the great truths of salvation that are at the heart of Christianity. 'We hold that a man is justified by faith apart from works of law' (3.28). This means that every Christian is released from guilt and fear. He can walk through life free and unafraid. I ended the last exposition by quoting, 'Nothing in my hand I bring.' Paul's gospel is that when we stand before the cross guilty and bankrupt, all the treasure of God's mercy is poured out upon us – just as we are. His love is free, and it is for sinners. We do not need to be good, or religious, or wise; we only need to trust him, to take him at his word, to let him be the pardoning God he wants to be.

> 'Tis mercy all, immense and free;
> For, O my God, it found out me!

The man who has discovered this and been liberated by it can never be the same again. If every Christian felt it burning in his bones the church would be revived.

5

Faith

1 What then shall we say about Abraham, our forefather according to the flesh? 2 For if Abraham was justified by works, he has something to boast about, but not before God. 3 For what does the scripture say? 'Abraham believed God, and it was reckoned to him as righteousness.' 4 Now to one who works, his wages are not reckoned as a gift but as his due. 5 And to one who does not work but trusts him who justifies the ungodly, his faith is reckoned as righteousness. 6 So also David pronounces a blessing upon the man to whom God reckons righteousness apart from works:

7 'Blessed are those whose iniquities are forgiven, and whose sins are covered;

8 blessed is the man against whom the Lord will not reckon his sin.'

9 Is this blessing pronounced only upon the circumcised, or also upon the uncircumcised? We say that faith was reckoned to Abraham as righteousness. 10 How then was it reckoned to him? Was it before or after he had been circumcised? It was not after, but before he was circumcised. 11 He received circumcision as a sign or seal of the righteousness which he had by faith while he was still uncircumcised. The purpose was to make him the father of all who believe without being circumcised and who thus have righteousness reckoned to them, 12 and likewise the father of the circumcised who are not merely circumcised but also follow the example of the faith which our father Abraham had before he was circumcised.

13 The promise to Abraham and his descendants, that they should inherit the world, did not come through the law but through the righteousness of faith. 14 If it is the adherents of the law who are to be the heirs, faith is null and the promise is void. 15 For the law brings wrath, but where there is no law there is no transgression.

16 That is why it depends on faith, in order that the promise may rest on grace and be guaranteed to all his descendants – not only to the adherents of the law but also to those who share the faith of Abraham, for he is the father of us all, 17 as it is written, 'I have

made you the father of many nations' – in the presence of the God in whom he believed, who gives life to the dead and calls into existence the things that do not exist. [18] In hope he believed against hope, that he should become the father of many nations; as he had been told, 'So shall your descendants be.' [19] He did not weaken in faith when he considered his own body, which was as good as dead because he was about a hundred years old, or when he considered the barrenness of Sarah's womb. [20] No distrust made him waver concerning the promise of God, but he grew strong in his faith as he gave glory to God, [21] fully convinced that God was able to do what he had promised. [22] That is why his faith was 'reckoned to him as righteousness'. [23] But the words, 'it was reckoned to him', were written not for his sake alone, [24] but for ours also. It will be reckoned to us who believe in him that raised from the dead Jesus our Lord, [25] who was put to death for our trespasses and raised for our justification.

Many people, reading the previous chapter (3.21–31), must have thought Paul had gone too far in his claim that it is by faith only, apart from any works done in obedience to the law, that man is justified. Perhaps he almost thought so himself; at all events, at the end of the paragraph he stops with a jerk to ask, 'What does all this amount to? Does it mean that the Old Testament law is now finished with for good and all?' (3.31). The question is a serious one, but the answer is a firm 'No'. On the contrary, the better you understand the gospel of God's gracious gift, the better you will understand the law, which tells of his command. 'We make the law firmer than ever.'

It is all very well to claim this; how can it be proved? There was no better way available than that of taking one of the outstanding characters of the Old Testament – Abraham (4.1). In fact, Paul may have had little choice about dealing with Abraham; his Jewish opponents probably threw the story of the great patriarch at his head. Look at Abraham, they said; there's a righteous man for you. He obeyed the law perfectly, even before it was given. (Some Jews actually said this.) He has something to boast about; what about works and faith now?

Paul begins his answer by quoting the Old Testament (4.3;

Genesis 15.6.) Abraham put his trust in God, and that was counted to him as righteousness. True, the Jew would answer; that makes my point. God rewarded him for his steadfast faithfulness (faith). But this, Paul replies (4.4, 5), is to get the whole picture wrong. Genesis is not speaking of a reward for work done, like the pay that an employer *owes* to an honest worker who does his duty. It is talking about a gift which God promised, and Abraham believed God would give him. Abraham did not earn it; he accepted it on trust. The very word 'counted' is significant. It is used again in the Old Testament, at Psalm 32.1, 2 (quoted in 4.7, 8). In this psalm, David does not speak of good men being paid for their goodness, but of bad men being forgiven their badness, which God does not 'count' against them. Abraham's faith meant his acceptance of God's gift of forgiveness, his trusting God to accept him. There is a further pointer to the truth here. When did Abraham get this blessing of forgiveness? When he was a circumcised Jew? No; for his faith and justification are mentioned in Genesis 15.6, but his circumcision not until Genesis 17.10 (4.10); circumcision came afterwards, as a seal of what God had already done (4.11).

So Abraham really is the father of the whole people of God – of Gentiles who believe, as he did, and also of Jews, who are not only circumcised but believers too (4.11, 12). As Paul is going to say later in the epistle, descent or succession from Abraham is nothing; faith, with God's call behind it, is everything.

So far the word 'faith' has been used a good deal, but it has not been explained. What does it mean? The answer to this is in two parts.

(1) Faith is the opposite of keeping the law and thereby earning salvation in terms of a sort of contract with God. An inheritance was promised to Abraham. Now a promise (unlike law) is not a contract. In a contract you do not trust your employer to give you your pay; you know that, provided you keep your side of the contract, he is legally bound to pay it. But all along the line in the story of Abraham we read of *promise*

and *trust*; there is thus no possible room for earning salvation by being obedient – unless indeed the very words 'faith' and 'promise' have lost their meaning (4.14).

(2) We still have not found a positive definition of faith. To get one Paul goes back once more to the story of Abraham. What was the promise made to Abraham? That he should be the ancestor of a multitude of nations (4.17). But this was unthinkable. Abraham was a hundred years old; his wife was ninety (Genesis 17.17); how could they have any children at all, not to speak of a large number of descendants? In circumstances like these you can look in one of two directions. You can look at the human situation; then indeed the outlook is black, and the situation hopeless. Or you can look at God, who gives the promise; and then there is hope, for God can raise the dead and create things out of nothing (4.17). This looking to God, which takes him at his word, is faith. It forgets the hopeless human circumstances, and rejoices in the power of God, which is able to overcome them all.

> Faith, mighty faith, the promise sees,
>   And looks to that alone;
> Laughs at impossibilities,
>   And cries: It shall be done! (4.20,21)

So Abraham is after all on the side of the gospel, because he helps us to see the real meaning of the Old Testament, which is not destroyed but fulfilled by Jesus Christ. The Old Testament law, *rightly understood*, is not against the gospel, but confirmed by it (3.31). Finally, Paul is able to wind up by showing (4.23–25) that all he has said about Abraham applies to us, since we too believe in a God who raises the dead. Only for us, who live after the resurrection of Jesus Christ, this truth is even clearer and more powerful.

6

5.1—11

Justification

1 Therefore, since we are justified by faith, we have peace with God through our Lord Jesus Christ. ² Through him we have obtained access to this grace in which we stand, and we rejoice in our hope of sharing the glory of God. ³ More than that, we rejoice in our sufferings, knowing that suffering produces endurance, ⁴ and endurance produces character, and character produces hope, ⁵ and hope does not disappoint us, because God's love has been poured into our hearts through the Holy Spirit which has been given to us.

6 While we were still weak, at the right time Christ died for the ungodly. ⁷ Why, one will hardly die for a righteous man – though perhaps for a good man one will dare even to die. ⁸ But God shows his love for us in that while we were yet sinners Christ died for us. ⁹ Since, therefore, we are now justified by his blood, much more shall we be saved by him from the wrath of God. ¹⁰ For if while we were enemies we were reconciled to God by the death of his Son, much more, now that we are reconciled, shall we be saved by his life. ¹¹ Not only so, but we also rejoice in God through our Lord Jesus Christ, through whom we have now received our reconciliation.

It is worth while to linger for a moment over the first verse of the next chapter. It takes justification (to which Paul has already devoted so much time and thought) for granted: Since then we have been justified by faith ... The chapter, as we shall see, goes on to query this assumption. Can we really believe that we have been justified? In view of our suffering? In view of our sin? We may question the assumption from another angle. Can a preacher, for example, really assume in these days that his congregation knows what justification means, and build, as Paul does, on that foundation? It is doubtful whether he can. 'Justification' is not one of the popular slogans of the present day, and is easily dismissed as irrelevant to modern man. Of course, the rather forbidding theological word does not matter; but the fact matters greatly, and the church's capacity for holiness and for evangelism turns upon our knowing what it is to be justified by grace and through faith.

There is another point to look at in the first verse. The RSV goes on: 'We have peace with God.' The RV has: 'Let us have peace with God.' The difference in Greek between 'we have' and 'let us have' amounts to only one letter, and in Paul's day the difference did not affect the pronunciation, so that slips could easily occur. But the difference in meaning is considerable, and the RSV translation is probably right. If we have been justified, we *are* at peace with God; justification is practically identical with reconciliation (see verses 9 and 10 below). If Paul *did* say, 'let us have', he must have meant, 'Let us continue at peace' (NEB), or better, 'Let us enjoy the peace we actually possess', for it does not rest with us whether we are at peace with God or not; it depends on God, who justifies men by his grace.

Justification means peace with God. What else? It would not be wrong to answer, everything else. It is best to look at the matter in this way. Before he became a Christian, Paul, like other Jews, believed that at the end of time God would hold a judgment. Those whom he acquitted (justified) would enter into the joy of the heavenly life. As a Christian Paul continued to believe in the last judgment (e.g. Romans 2.5); but he now knew that to believers God had given the verdict of acquittal (justification) by anticipation. From this it follows that believers through their justification enter here and now into an anticipation of the heavenly life – into the life which is righteousness, peace, and joy in the Holy Spirit (Romans 14.17). This is why justification is so important; it is not itself the whole of Christianity, but it is the point on which everything else – the new life, and heaven itself – depends.

From this point we can go on to understand the rest of the paragraph. It faces up to difficulties which might seem to deny the truth that God has justified us. Take suffering, for example. Does not suffering make it impossible to believe in the justifying love of God? No, says Paul; on the contrary we can even glory in our suffering. He argues this out in verses 3, 4, 5. Afflictions do not contradict our hope, for God uses them for our benefit. Affliction results in endurance, the power to look beyond the present into God's future; endurance produces tried character, and tried character confirms our hope. But suppose this hope is simply deluded, says the doubter. Far from it, for it is not mere hope, but rests on what God has already done for us. He has poured out (compare Acts 2.17; Joel 2.28) his Spirit, and thereby filled our hearts with love, which transforms them, and brings them into harmony with what God intends (Romans 13.8–10). If God has done this, can we think that he will fail to complete his purpose for us?

There is a harder problem. Can I believe in the justifying love of God when I consider my sins? This is a serious query, but it misunderstands the whole situation. Look at a human analogy, says Paul. You would scarcely bring yourself to die for a righteous man, would you? Well, perhaps for a really good man you might make the sacrifice (verse 7). But now see what Christ has done. We were neither good nor righteous, but still sinners when Christ died for us (verse 8). In face of that, how can you doubt the love of God, or deny that it is love *for sinners*? In face of such an overwhelming demonstration you must admit this fundamental fact. And if you admit this, you must go further (verses 9 and 10, in which Paul puts the same truth twice over). Through the death of his Son God has justified us, reconciled us – brought us back into right relations with himself. But a dead Christ is not God's last word. Christ is alive. And if his death meant so much, what will his life mean but full and final salvation? Here Paul's thought is running on into the vision of our eternal life with God; but he has not forgotten the present. If God has so dealt with the past; if he has so secured the future; if he has set his love beyond any shadow of doubt; then indeed we can rejoice in God (verse 11).

Again, Paul has brought us to the core of our faith, and shown us the secret of the Christian life. How different from our narrow and nervous religion, our proud and petty piety! Nothing but this will set us free from ourselves to glorify God and serve our neighbours.

5.12–21

So Wide...

12 Therefore as sin came into the world through one man and death through sin, and so death spread to all men because all men sinned – ¹³sin indeed was in the world before the law was given, but sin is not counted where there is no law. ¹⁴Yet death reigned from Adam to Moses, even over those whose sins were not like the transgression of Adam, who was a type of the one who was to come.

15 But the free gift is not like the trespass. For if many died through one man's trespass, much more have the grace of God and the free gift in the grace of that one man Jesus Christ abounded for many. ¹⁶And the free gift is not like the effect of that one man's sin. For the judgment following one trespass brought condemnation, but the free gift following many trespasses brings justification. ¹⁷If, because of one man's trespass, death reigned through that one man, much more will those who receive the abundance of grace and the free gift of righteousness reign in life through the one man Jesus Christ.

18 Then as one man's trespass led to condemnation for all men, so one man's act of righteousness leads to acquittal and life for all men. ¹⁹For as by one man's disobedience many were made sinners, so by one man's obedience many will be made righteous. ²⁰Law came in, to increase the trespass; but where sin increased, grace abounded all the more, ²¹so that, as sin reigned in death, grace also might reign through righteousness to eternal life through Jesus Christ our Lord.

In the preceding paragraph (5.1–11) we saw Paul facing the questions, Can I really believe that God will justify one who is a sinner? Can I believe in God's justifying love in the face of suffering? The new paragraph deals with the last question a man can ask: Can I really believe that God's love is for *me*? Can I believe that he will justify *me*? No doubt this gospel of God's grace applies to some people – to those, perhaps, who are naturally good, or naturally religious; to great men, like Paul himself, or Luther, or Wesley. But is it reasonable to suppose that it applies to an insignificant, not to say sinful, person like me?

The essence of the answer is that the gospel is as wide in its scope as the human race itself. This is the point of the reference to Adam (5.14). The human race is one, and its redeemer is one. Where sin abounded, grace much more abounded (5.20); wherever there is sin (and that is everywhere), there is grace, and there is always more grace than there is sin. There is room for everyone; the love of God is broad –

> So wide it never passed by one,
> Or it had passed by me.

Because it covers the whole race, it includes me.

This is the essence of the matter. But there are details to take up. Sin is as universal as grace, and the wages of sin is death (6.23). But what is sin? The opening verses (5.12–14) are instructive, but by no means easy. Paul tells his story in terms of the first three chapters of Genesis. The truth that he finds in these chapters is religious and theological truth, and is in no way invalidated by changing scientific views of the origin of the universe and of human life. The name Adam in Hebrew means 'man', and what Paul shows us is the story of *man* – whether or not we can think of it as being also the story of the first man. No sooner does man turn away from God than he finds himself cut off from the only source of life. He is thus under sentence of death. From the beginning he has been under this sentence, because from the beginning he has turned away from God, but this fact has only been visible when some divine command, whether God's simple command to Adam or the long and complicated law given to Moses, has been in operation. Paul uses a commercial metaphor: just as you cannot enter a man's wealth in a ledger unless you have a unit of currency, so you cannot reckon up sin unless there is a law to turn sin into actual transgression (5.13). We shall come back to the law later (5.20 and chapter 7).

It is in this setting that Paul says of Adam that he was a figure of the one who was to come (5.14). The father of the race, by the act he committed, affected all those who came after him; Jesus also, by his act, affected all mankind. The two stand in corresponding positions. It is at first sight surprising that Paul, after saying this, should proceed to describe differences between Adam and Christ. These run through verses 15, 16, 17: '*Not like* the trespass ... *much more* ... *not like* the effect of that one man's sin ... *much more* ...' We do not reach parallel statements until we come to verses 18 and 19: '*As* one man's trespass ... *so* ... *as* by one man's disobedience ... *so* ...' This fact, puzzling at first, is very suggestive. If the verses (18, 19) that express resemblance are examined, we find that the words used to describe what Jesus did are 'act of righteousness' and 'obedience'. If we turn back to verses 15, 16 and 17, we find different words: 'grace', 'free gift'. Looked at from one angle, Jesus was a man like Adam, except that where Adam was disobedient he was obedient. Looked at from another angle, Jesus was completely unlike Adam, because he was not man but God, who acts in grace and gives gifts to men.

There is one more thing in the chapter to account for. Paul makes a plain comparison and contrast between Adam and Christ. Adam made things go wrong: Christ put them right. In this process, where does the law (which meant so much to Jews like Paul) come in? It comes in in verse 20, not on equal terms, but in a subordinate position. It slipped into this position, as it were, by the back door (Paul uses the same word of the false brethren in Galatians 2.4). This is not Paul's last word about the law; but he is quite clear that it is not the same as gospel. In fact, law does not stop sin; it tends rather to increase it (5.20); but we shall come back to this in chapter 7.

Paul sums up in verse 21. The reign of grace, which means eternal life, is as wide and certain as the reign of sin. Any one who knows that he is a sinner, who has been condemned by the law, can be sure that God's grace is for him. No one is left out. It was to call sinners like us that Jesus Christ came from heaven (Mark 2.17). As Luther says on Galatians 2.20 (*He loved me and gave himself for me*): 'Read with great vehemency these words, "me", and "for me", and so inwardly practise with thyself, that thou, with a sure faith, mayst conceive and print this "me" in thy heart, and apply it unto thyself, not doubting but that thou art of the number of those to whom this "me" belongeth.'

8 6.1–23

The New Life

1 What shall we say then? Are we to continue in sin that grace may abound? ²By no means! How can we who died to sin still live in it? ³Do you not know that all of us who have been baptized into Christ Jesus were baptized into his death? ⁴We were buried therefore with him by baptism into death, so that as Christ was raised from the dead by the glory of the Father, we too might walk in newness of life.

5 For if we have been united with him in a death like his, we shall certainly be united with him in a resurrection like his. ⁶We know that our old self was crucified with him so that the sinful body might be destroyed, and we might no longer be enslaved to sin. ⁷For he who has died is freed from sin. ⁸But if we have died with Christ, we believe that we shall also live with him. ⁹For we know that Christ being raised from the dead will never die again; death no longer has dominion over him. ¹⁰The death he died he died to sin, once for all, but the life he lives he lives to God. ¹¹So you also must consider yourselves dead to sin and alive to God in Christ Jesus.

12 Let not sin therefore reign in your mortal bodies, to make you obey their passions. ¹³Do not yield your members to sin as instruments of wickedness, but yield yourselves to God as men who have been brought from death to life, and your members to God as instruments of righteousness. ¹⁴For sin will have no dominion over you, since you are not under law but under grace.

15 What then? Are we to sin because we are not under law but under grace? By no means! ¹⁶Do you not know that if you yield yourselves to any one as obedient slaves, you are slaves of the one whom you obey, either of sin, which leads to death, or of obedience, which leads to righteousness? ¹⁷But thanks be to God, that you who were once slaves of sin have become obedient from the heart to the standard of teaching to which you were committed, ¹⁸and, having been set free from sin, have become slaves of righteousness. ¹⁹I am speaking in human terms, because of your natural limitations. For just as you once yielded your members to impurity and to greater

and greater iniquity, so now yield your members to righteousness for sanctification.

20 When you were slaves of sin, you were free in regard to righteousness. 21 But then what return did you get from the things of which you are now ashamed? The end of those things is death. 22 But now that you have been set free from sin and have become slaves of God, the return you get is sanctification and its end, eternal life. 23 For the wages of sin is death, but the free gift of God is eternal life in Christ Jesus our Lord.

Chapter 5 came to a triumphant conclusion. Our justification by God is secure. Sin cannot stop it; suffering does not contradict it. It avails for all, the whole family of Adam. So great is God's grace, that however sin may multiply grace will always multiply much more (5.20). This is one of the points in the epistle (compare 3.31; 7.7; 9.6, 14; 11.1) where Paul seems to pause, almost as if he wondered whether perhaps he had gone too far. If it be true that the more sin man contributes to the world situation, the more grace abounds, then surely there is a case for sinning as much as possible – it will give God so much more opportunity of showing his forgiving love. 'What shall we say then? Are we to continue in sin that grace may abound?' (6.1). To such a suggestion Paul can return only a 'By no means!' When God acts in grace it is certainly not with the intention that sin should go on, much less that it should increase. Paul, however, is not content simply to say that sin is a bad thing, and that God wills that it should cease; he argues the situation out, with the result that we have in chapter 6 a very important account of the new life (6.4) Christians are called to live.

To suggest that Christians should willingly continue in sin is sheer nonsense. How did you enter the Christian life? Paul asks. It was by death, and the death was a death to sin; clearly you cannot go on living in sin (6.2). But this is the statement Paul needs to explain, and we shall follow out his explanation, altering the order a little in the interests of clarity.

First, and most important, before any religious or moral experience of ours, there happened the death and resurrection of Jesus – always the central events in Paul's mind. What sort of death did Jesus die? He died a death that was the perfect consummation of a life in which sin had no place. He died *to sin* (6.10) – because he would not compromise with sin, and because sin killed him. This was not the end: God raised him from the dead (6.4); his life of perfect goodness was vindicated and renewed, so that he lives *to God* (6.10) – only God could raise up a dead body, and in his new resurrection life, as previously, Jesus lives in perfect obedience to and harmony with the Father. Paul has not finished his argument, but he has taken a long step. If Christianity depends on the death and resurrection of Jesus, then certainly it can have no truck with sin.

Paul goes on. The death and resurrection of Jesus are as definitely events in history as the Battle of Waterloo; but they are more than this. Each Christian believer enters into them, and, as it were, lives them over again. Paul expresses this by reference to baptism, which, in his day, suggested not a rite performed on infants too young to reason, but a fully conscious part of the conversion experience of adult believers. Baptism, which meant real immersion, or *burying* under the water, and again a rising up out of the water, was well fitted to represent what happens to a man united by faith with the crucified, buried, and risen Christ. We died, and were buried with Christ (Paul says this repeatedly – verses 3, 4, 5, 6, 7, 8). So if he died to sin, we have died to sin too. But if we have died with Christ, we shall also be raised with Christ (6.4, 5, 8), and the life he lives to God, we too shall live. Shall we then continue in sin? What nonsense!

One point, however, Paul insists on. There is no automatic process (baptism or anything else) that relieves a Christian of the responsibility for putting into practice what has already happened to him in principle. If you have been joined by faith with the death and resurrection of Jesus, then you must no longer allow your members to be used in the service of sin; you must use them for God in the service of righteousness

32

(6.13). This will be possible, because your relation with God is governed not by your obedience to law, but by his grace (6.14).

This is a daring thing to say, and immediately an objection arises (perhaps from the back of Paul's own mind, perhaps from a heckler). If we are no longer under the law (which forbids sin) we can do what we like; we can sin as much as we please! (6.15). It is a similar point to that of 6.1, and it gets the same answer: By no means! It leads Paul, however, to make clear the place of obedience in the Christian life. Faith is not inconsistent with obedience; on the contrary, faith demands it. We remember how Paul speaks of the 'obedience of faith', at 1.5. All life is obedience, or servitude; and the question is whether man will be the slave of sin, or of righteousness (6.16). Paul knows how this issue has been settled for his readers. Once they had been slaves of sin and uncleanness, but now (compare 6.13) they have given themselves to God (6.17). Note how Paul puts the matter in this verse: the Romans had become obedient to the gospel message they had heard. It could not be more plainly stated that God himself is present in the preaching of his word.

Paul sums up the argument in 6.23: Work for sin, and you will be paid – with death; you can never serve God well enough to merit a reward, but he will freely give eternal life to those who serve him. The issue before man is nothing less than – life or death.

9 7.1–25

What is Religion?

1 Do you not know, brethren – for I am speaking to those who know the law – that the law is binding on a person only during his life? ²Thus a married woman is bound by law to her husband as long as he lives; but if her husband dies she is discharged from the law concerning the husband. ³Accordingly, she will be called an adulteress if she lives with another man while her husband is alive. But if her husband dies she is free from that law, and if she marries another man she is not an adulteress.

4 Likewise, my brethren, you have died to the law through the body of Christ, so that you may belong to another, to him who has been raised from the dead in order that we may bear fruit for God. ⁵While we were living in the flesh, our sinful passions, aroused by the law, were at work in our members to bear fruit for death. ⁶But now we are discharged from the law, dead to that which held us captive, so that we serve not under the old written code but in the new life of the Spirit.

7 What then shall we say? That the law is sin? By no means! Yet, if it had not been for the law, I should not have known sin. I should not have known what it is to covet if the law had not said, 'You shall not covet.' ⁸But sin, finding opportunity in the commandment, wrought in me all kinds of covetousness. Apart from the law sin lies dead. ⁹I was once alive apart from the law, but when the commandment came, sin revived and I died; ¹⁰the very commandment which promised life proved to be death to me. ¹¹For sin, finding opportunity in the commandment, deceived me and by it killed me. ¹²So the law is holy, and the commandment is holy and just and good.

13 Did that which is good, then, bring death to me? By no means! It was sin, working death in me through what is good, in order that sin might be shown to be sin, and through the commandment might become sinful beyond measure. ¹⁴We know that the law is spiritual; but I am carnal, sold under sin. ¹⁵I do not understand my own actions. For I do not do what I want, but I do the very thing I hate. ¹⁶Now if I do what I do not want, I agree that the law is good. ¹⁷So then

it is no longer I that do it, but sin which dwells within me. [18]For I know that nothing good dwells within me, that is, in my flesh. I can will what is right, but I cannot do it. [19]For I do not do the good I want, but the evil I do not want is what I do. [20]Now if I do what I do not want, it is no longer I that do it, but sin which dwells within me.

21 So I find it to be a law that when I want to do right, evil lies close at hand. [22]For I delight in the law of God, in my inmost self, [23]but I see in my members another law at war with the law of my mind and making me captive to the law of sin which dwells in my members. [24]Wretched man that I am! Who will deliver me from this body of death? [25]Thanks be to God through Jesus Christ our Lord! So then, I of myself serve the law of God with my mind, but with my flesh I serve the law of sin.

The last main point handled in chapter 6 was this: The gospel has nothing to do with disobedience; there is no question of going on in sin in order to encourage God to be gracious. The members which have so long been abandoned to the service of sin must be wrenched away and offered to God in obedience. But this gospel obedience, the obedience of faith (1.5), is a new kind of obedience, which is quite independent of law (in the sense of legalism). Christians have nothing to do with legalism, and so far as this is what 'law' means, or can be taken to mean, they have finished with it altogether. It is this point that Paul goes on to develop in 7.1–6.

He uses an analogy. Take the case of a married woman (7.2). In one respect at least, she is, in virtue of her marriage, no longer free: she is debarred from sexual union with any man other than her husband. Such union means adultery (7.3). Only one thing can end this situation: the death of her husband. If this takes place, she is free. This (says Paul) is like our relation with the law. Only one thing could free us from it – death. It is true that the parallel is not exact, for the law did not die; it is Christ who died, and we with him. But the result is plain: we are dead to the law, and as far as we are concerned it is dead and done with, and we are free – free, of course, for service. Our relation with God is based no longer on legalism, but on something quite different (7.4, 6).

35

Here is another of the places (compare 6.1) where Paul seems to check himself. Has he gone too far? Has he committed himself to saying that the law of Moses is actually sinful? This he certainly does not mean (7.7). The law stands written in the Old Testament. It is part of the oracles of God (3.2). Because it is from God it is spiritual (7.14). As God's utterance it is holy, and the commandments God has given are holy, they require the right thing, and they are kindly intended because they come from his grace (7.12). All this is important, and Paul lays great stress upon it. The Christian church can never rid itself of the Old Testament. Yet, when all this has been said, it remains true that the law has somehow got itself mixed up with sin to such an extent as almost to cease to be itself (7.7–11).

If it were not for the law, says Paul, I should know nothing about sin (7.7). There are several points behind this. First – the law, by giving specific commands, which can be broken, makes sin knowable (compare 3.20; 5.13). Secondly, as every schoolboy knows, laws invite rebellion; there is pleasure in breaking rules. But, thirdly, there is a deeper connection between sin and law than this. The law states God's absolute claim upon his creature, man; but it states it in terms of particular requirements, and the result of this is that man, who has in him a twist towards evil, begins to think, 'If I can fulfil these requirements, I shall have done all God wants, and he will be bound to reward me.' Man keeps the law, as Paul had done (Philippians 3.6), but for the wrong reason; and so (7.7) the law which had said 'Thou shalt not desire' (Exodus 20.17) provoked all kinds of desire (7.8) – not simply desire for one's neighbour's house or wife, but the far more deadly desire to gain control of God by paying him his fee.

This dreadful perversion of the law, the highest religion men had known before Christ, was the work of sin (7.11, 13, 17, 20), which had entered the world through Adam (5.12), and nothing could have shown up so clearly the wickedness of this God-opposing force (7.13). Law was not made for this situation. It was intended to lead to life (7.10), but it was not designed for a world in which sin had broken loose. To deal with such a desperate position something more was needed – as we shall see (7.25).

Paul goes on to analyse further the effect sin has upon the law. There is a good and holy divine law; but sin has produced a counterfeit copy of this law, something that looks like the good religion of the Old Testament but is in effect the law that belongs to sin and death (7.23, 25; 8.2). It looks like the good Old Testament religion, because those who practise it observe the ceremonies of the Pentateuch; but it belongs to sin and leads to death, because they are keeping the rules for the wrong reason. They are keeping them not out of pure and grateful love to God, but with a view to winning reward for themselves. This lies behind Paul's confession, 'I do not do the good I want, but the evil I do not want is what I do' (7.19, and other verses). This does not mean that he can do nothing but wicked things; it means that even when he does good things he does them wrongly – for the wrong motives and in a wrong relation with God.

From this situation, in which sin corrupts the best of human endeavour, man has no power to free himself. There is only one hope. We are to hear much more of it later (and we have heard much already); in this paragraph there is nothing but a thanksgiving, but that is enough: Thanks be to God through Jesus Christ our Lord! (7.25).

Chapter 7 is often taken as the story of Paul's conversion, but it is something deeper than that. Not only at his conversion but throughout his life, and throughout eternity, Paul depends absolutely on Christ. All Christians must remember this. The practice of religion – even of Judaism, or Christianity – cannot save a man. Every moment he must depend on Jesus, and Jesus only.

10 8.1–11

Life in the Spirit

1 There is therefore now no condemnation for those who are in Christ Jesus. ²For the law of the Spirit of life in Christ Jesus has set me free from the law of sin and death. ³For God has done what the law, weakened by the flesh, could not do: sending his own Son in the likeness of sinful flesh and for sin, he condemned sin in the flesh, ⁴in order that the just requirement of the law might be fulfilled in us, who walk not according to the flesh but according to the Spirit. ⁵For those who live according to the flesh set their minds on the things of the flesh, but those who live according to the Spirit set their minds on the things of the Spirit. ⁶To set the mind on the flesh is death, but to set the mind on the Spirit is life and peace. ⁷For the mind that is set on the flesh is hostile to God; it does not submit to God's law, indeed it cannot; ⁸and those who are in the flesh cannot please God.

9 But you are not in the flesh, you are in the Spirit, if in fact the Spirit of God dwells in you. Any one who does not have the Spirit of Christ does not belong to him. ¹⁰But if Christ is in you, although your bodies are dead because of sin, your spirits are alive because of righteousness. ¹¹If the Spirit of him who raised Jesus from the dead dwells in you, he who raised Christ Jesus from the dead will give life to your mortal bodies also through his Spirit which dwells in you.

This short paragraph links up more closely with 7.1–6 than with 7.7–25, which, as we have seen, deals with a special problem. In 7.1–6 Paul spoke so emphatically about Christian freedom from the law that he evidently felt obliged to turn aside to show that the Old Testament truly was God's word, and a good gift to man, even though sin had abused and perverted it. In chapter 8 he comes back to the theme of Christian freedom.

Verse 1 restates the central theme of justification in a new way, using the expression 'in Christ' instead of faith. 'In Christ' describes the objective fact, faith the way in which the fact is grasped. Christ took affliction and judgment upon himself, and passed triumphantly through to be vindicated in the resurrection. Any one who is *in him* has had God's judgment anticipated for him, and because he has a righteousness not his own but Christ's, the judgment must be favourable. He is free from condemnation, not because he is a good, religious man, but because God sees him in Christ –

> Alive in him, my living head,
> And clothed in righteousness divine.

In verse 2 we again meet with two laws, as we did in 7.21–23. The word 'law' as Paul uses it here means what it meant to a Jew – a way of life, and especially a religious way of life. The 'law of sin and death' means the way of legalism, which God's law becomes when it is perverted by sin and thus ends in death. This is not what God intended that his law should be, but the divine way of obedience only achieves its goal through the work of the life-giving Spirit, and in Christ. It is no exaggeration to say that this verse contains a complete picture of the Christian life as Paul understood it. Negatively, it is the end of legalism, of the eternally unsuccessful attempt to please God by our own efforts, which can end only in failure, and thus in condemnation and death. Positively, it is life in Christ, united with him by faith, and quickened by the Spirit. Paul states the matter here in terms that apply in the first instance to the individual, but 'in Christ' and 'the Spirit' both represent truths that can reach complete fulfilment only in fellowship and community.

Verse 2 thus describes the Christian life as Christians live it, free from the law and open to God's grace. But how can men live such a life? Can they simply make up their minds to change their ways, and be different from what they were before? Paul knows very well that they cannot. Behind the liberation that every believer experiences lies a deed that only God could do. This is described in verse 3: 'For God has done what the law, weakened by the flesh, could not do: sending his own Son . . .'

There was nothing wrong with the law in itself. Paul has been at great pains to show this, and here he repeats his conclusion. The fault is not in the law but in the circumstances in which it has been used. Men have tried to make it a way of salvation, which it is not and never can be. If it were not for the flesh, the law might regulate man's walk with God; but the flesh is there, all the time drawing man away from God. So God did what the law could not do. For all his efforts, man, even religious man, could not make his way to God; God therefore came to man, and came to man precisely as he is. He sent his Son, and sent him to share the same sinful humanity that we all have. Not that Christ was sinful; he was not. Only he was sinless, not because he had some unfair advantage over the rest of men, but because his divine power constantly overcame the real inclination, the temptation to sin, which he shared with the rest of us. Thus he came *for* sin (that is, to deal with sin), and he condemned sin in the very place where it reigned – in the flesh.

It has been necessary to explain these first three verses in some detail. The rest of the paragraph is equally important, but it can be dealt with quickly. The practical point in it is this. God could (we may suppose) have dealt with the world's sin by turning it off, as with a tap. He did not do this, but sent his Son into the rough and tumble of human existence, into the world of sin and death, there to grapple with and defeat those two alien powers. This means that it is now open to men to live 'according to the flesh' or 'according to the Spirit' (capital S – the Spirit of God is meant, not man's human spirit). Living 'according to the flesh' does not necessarily mean living a sensual life (NEB's 'our lower nature' is misleading), but a life that seeks its fulfilment in itself, possibly in a very aesthetic and 'spiritual' sense; living 'according to the Spirit' means a life that has its meaning and its springs in God. Paul is gripped by the sense of urgency that arises from the conviction that life 'according to the flesh' can lead only to death (8.6). It is a grim urgency that we might with advantage rediscover.

If God is For Us . . .

12 So then, brethren, we are debtors, not to the flesh, to live according to the flesh – [13] for if you live according to the flesh you will die, but if by the Spirit you put to death the deeds of the body you will live. [14] For all who are led by the Spirit of God are sons of God. [15] For you did not receive the spirit of slavery to fall back into fear, but you have received the spirit of sonship. When we cry, 'Abba! Father!' [16] it is the Spirit himself bearing witness with our spirit that we are children of God, [17] and if children, then heirs, heirs of God and fellow heirs with Christ, provided we suffer with him in order that we may also be glorified with him.

18 I consider that the sufferings of this present time are not worth comparing with the glory that is to be revealed to us. [19] For the creation waits with eager longing for the revealing of the sons of God; [20] for the creation was subjected to futility, not of its own will but by the will of him who subjected it in hope; [21] because the creation itself will be set free from its bondage to decay and obtain the glorious liberty of the children of God. [22] We know that the whole creation has been groaning in travail together until now; [23] and not only the creation, but we ourselves, who have the first fruits of the Spirit, groan inwardly as we wait for adoption as sons, the redemption of our bodies. [24] For in this hope we were saved. Now hope that is seen is not hope. For who hopes for what he sees? [25] But if we hope for what we do not see, we wait for it with patience.

26 Likewise the Spirit helps us in our weakness; for we do not know how to pray as we ought, but the Spirit himself intercedes for us with sighs too deep for words. [27] And he who searches the hearts of men knows what is the mind of the Spirit, because the Spirit intercedes for the saints according to the will of God.

28 We know that in everything God works for good with those who love him, who are called according to his purpose. [29] For those whom he foreknew he also predestined to be conformed to the image of his Son, in order that he might be the first-born among many

brethren. [30] And those whom he predestined he also called; and those whom he called he also justified; and those whom he justified he also glorified.

[31] What then shall we say to this? If God is for us, who is against us? [32] He who did not spare his own Son but gave him up for us all, will he not also give us all things with him? [33] Who shall bring any charge against God's elect? It is God who justifies; [34] who is to condemn? Is it Christ Jesus, who died, yes, who was raised from the dead, who is at the right hand of God, who indeed intercedes for us? [35] Who shall separate us from the love of Christ? Shall tribulation, or distress, or persecution, or famine, or nakedness, or peril, or sword? [36] As it is written,

> 'For thy sake we are being killed all the day long;
> we are regarded as sheep to be slaughtered.'

[37] No, in all these things we are more than conquerors through him who loved us. [38] For I am sure that neither death, nor life, nor angels, nor principalities, nor things present, nor things to come, nor powers, [39] nor height, nor depth, nor anything else in all creation, will be able to separate us from the love of God in Christ Jesus our Lord.

If what Paul has said up to this point is true, what sort of life will Christians lead? What is it that Paul, and his first-century Roman readers, and his twentieth-century British readers, have received from God, and can in turn offer to the world? The remainder of Romans 8 is part of the answer to these questions. It is a wonderful chapter, but we must not lose our heads about it, or read it in isolation from all that Paul tells us in chapters 3 and 5 of the deeds of God, and in chapters 12 and 13 of the way of Christian obedience.

Paul does not lose his head; he begins with his feet firmly planted on the earth. The Christian life is a life of obligation. We are debtors (8.12). To whom am I in debt? The normal human answer is: Myself. 'I owe it to myself', we say, 'to do this or that.' Not so Paul. That is 'living according to the flesh' (8.13), and if you do it, you will die. The way to life is through death. This is just what Jesus had said (Mark 8.34, 35) about denying yourself and taking up the cross, though put in new words. This is the way to life, not by a psychological trick, but because it is the way God's Spirit works, and to be led by the Spirit is to be a child of God (8.14).

There are few Christian doctrines so puzzling as the doctrine of the Holy Spirit, and the best clue to it is given in the next few verses. To receive the Spirit does not mean (as a religion of legalism does mean) bondage and fear; the Spirit is the Spirit of adoption, who makes us God's children, and makes us know that we are God's children. It is the Spirit that makes us cry out to God, Abba, Father (8.15). It is worthwhile to linger over this word *Abba*. It is not Greek, but Aramaic, the language Jesus normally used. In that language it was not used for formal, liturgical purposes; it was the word a boy would use at home when he addressed his father in the familiar friendly way. But Jesus used it when he spoke to God (Mark 14.36), and Christians use it after him. Our adoption is not a matter of the liturgical service-book, but of the intimate life of God's family.

This, however, is where we must pause for a moment. Look on to verse 23, and you will see that our adoption is something that has not yet happened. We are waiting for it. But in verse 15 it has so surely happened that already we are calling God Abba. It is through the Holy Spirit that both these statements can be true. God has not yet brought his story to its close. Verse 18 looks forward to the glory that is to be revealed, and Paul never wavers in his forward look; the present is a time of suffering, of unanswered questions, of unsolved problems, and the time is still to come when God will set all creation free from its bondage to corruption (8.21). But here and now, through the Spirit, God does something that brings the glorious future into the present – adoption, for example. What God has planned for those who love him far surpasses our dreams; but the Spirit teaches us what can be known of it in this world (compare 1 Corinthians 2.9, 10). The very word 'first fruits' applied to the Spirit in 8.23 makes the point. The gift of the Spirit, given here and now to God's people, is the pledge and sample of the full harvest that is to come in God's future.

For us now the words are hope, and patient endurance (8.24, 25) – endurance made possible through the Spirit's help. How much we need it! By ourselves we cannot manage the most elementary religious duties; we do not even know how to say our prayers. But with the Spirit's aid we need no fine words; the Spirit himself is God, and prayers that he inspires God cannot fail to hear (8.26, 27).

This brings Paul back to his anchorage. No man has ever experienced the gospel more vividly and fervently than he did; but he knows that it depends not on his feelings but on God. So, in verses 28–30, he returns to God's eternal purpose. What God set out to produce was a large family, all bearing his image, with Christ as their elder brother; this purpose he is working out, from foreknowledge, through justification, to glory. He is doing this for us, rebellious wretches, who have no claim on anything but his wrath. Who can believe it? Who can fail to believe it? says Paul (8.31–34). If God could give us his Son, what will he keep back? If God is on our side, who can be against us? And he is on our side; he has proved it by the love he commends in the death of his Son (5.8). God – on our side! We ought to have been on his, but we failed him. And now, because he will not give us up, he has taken our part, and taken our sins upon himself.

If God has thus resolved to win men out of their disobedience and into eternal fellowship with himself, all the rest (8.31–39) follows. What can separate us from his love? There is persecution; but the very fact that Paul can speak of this in Old Testament language (verse 36) shows that God has allowed for it, and is not going to be beaten by it. There are all the spiritual powers of earth and hell; there are the thousand uncertainties of life; and there is the last grand certainty of death. But how can any of these separate us from him who is as truly Lord as he is love?

I have several times in these pages quoted the Wesley hymns in order to bring out Paul's meaning. This chapter could have been filled with hymns, for though the Wesleys were at home everywhere in the Bible, it was to Romans 8 that they constantly returned. It is hard to choose; but let this translation of John's put the emphasis where it belongs – on the unfathomable and eternal mercy of God.

Fixed on this ground will I remain,
    Though my heart fail and flesh decay;
This anchor shall my soul sustain,
    When earth's foundations melt away;
    Mercy's full power I then shall prove,
    Loved with an everlasting love.

The People of God

1 I am speaking the truth in Christ, I am not lying; my conscience bears me witness in the Holy Spirit, ²that I have great sorrow and unceasing anguish in my heart. ³For I could wish that I myself were accursed and cut off from Christ for the sake of my brethren, my kinsmen by race. ⁴They are Israelites, and to them belong the sonship, the glory, the covenants, the giving of the law, the worship, and the promises; ⁵to them belong the patriarchs, and of their race, according to the flesh, is the Christ. God who is over all be blessed for ever. Amen.

6 But it is not as though the word of God had failed. For not all who are descended from Israel belong to Israel, ⁷and not all are children of Abraham because they are his descendants; but 'Through Isaac shall your descendants be named.' ⁸This means that it is not the children of the flesh who are the children of God, but the children of the promise are reckoned as descendants. ⁹For this is what the promise said, 'About this time I will return and Sarah shall have a son.' ¹⁰And not only so, but also when Rebecca had conceived children by one man, our forefather Isaac, ¹¹though they were not yet born and had done nothing either good or bad, in order that God's purpose of election might continue, not because of works but because of his call, ¹²she was told, 'The elder will serve the younger.' ¹³As it is written, 'Jacob I loved, but Esau I hated.'

14 What shall we say then? Is there injustice on God's part? By no means! ¹⁵For he says to Moses, 'I will have mercy on whom I have mercy, and I will have compassion on whom I have compassion.' ¹⁶So it depends not upon man's will or exertion, but upon God's mercy. ¹⁷For the scripture says to Pharaoh, 'I have raised you up for the very purpose of showing my power in you, so that my name may be proclaimed in all the earth.' ¹⁸So then he has mercy upon whomever he wills, and he hardens the heart of whomever he wills.

19 You will say to me then, 'Why does he still find fault? For who can resist his will?' ²⁰But who are you, a man, to answer back to

God? Will what is moulded say to its moulder, 'Why have you made me thus?' [21] Has the potter no right over the clay, to make out of the same lump one vessel for beauty and another for menial use? [22] What if God, desiring to show his wrath and to make known his power, has endured with much patience the vessels of wrath made for destruction, [23] in order to make known the riches of his glory for the vessels of mercy, which he has prepared beforehand for glory, [24] even us whom he has called, not from the Jews only but also from the Gentiles? [25] As indeed he says in Hosea,

'Those who were not my people
I will call "my people",
and her who was not beloved
I will call "my beloved".'

[26] 'And in the very place where it was said to them, "You are not my people",
they will be called "sons of the living God".'

[27] And Isaiah cries out concerning Israel: 'Though the number of the sons of Israel be as the sand of the sea, only a remnant of them will be saved; [28] for the Lord will execute his sentence upon the earth with rigour and despatch.' [29] And as Isaiah predicted,

'If the Lord of hosts had not left us children,
we would have fared like Sodom and been made like Gomorrah.'

It is told of Alexander Whyte that once, when he was preaching, ' "What will it be to be there!" he exclaimed at the close of a rapturous passage on the bliss of the redeemed; and then, suddenly and solemnly, he added, "And what will it be NOT to be there!" ' The change from the eighth to the ninth chapter of Romans is like that. You cannot paint the last paragraph of Romans 8 in colours that are too bright; you can only join Paul in giving glory to God for his unspeakable gift. But as you join him, you can see the cloud pass over his face. What about those, the Jews, to whom the unspeakable gift was first offered? They have turned their back on it. They were Paul's own people, his own flesh and blood. More than that, they were God's own people. Everything that could have been done to prepare them for their supreme privilege, he had done for them. Out of Egypt God had called his son (Hosea 11.1); his glory had gone before them in the pillars of cloud and fire (Exodus 13.21); He had made his covenants with them, and given them the law, the temple-worship, and the prophetic promises. He had raised up Christ himself as one of themselves (9.4, 5); yet they had rejected him. He came to his own, and his own did not receive him (John 1.11). No wonder Paul was racked with grief and ceaseless pain (9.2), willing to suffer a curse if his brethren might be saved (9.3). And if it was bad for Paul, what must it have been like for God, as the Gentile world accepted the Gospel, and the Jews turned it down?

There was no denying the facts; they unfolded themselves in the advancing Christian mission. What conclusion was to be drawn from them? Paul mentions one possible conclusion in verse 6: God's word, his promise to Israel, has broken down. He planned and promised what he could not fulfil. Of course, Paul could not believe that this was true. But if it was not true, what was one to do? Paul's answer was to analyse the meaning of God's promise. It was spoken to Israel; but what do you mean by Israel? If you mean all who belong by blood to the race of Israel, then certainly the promise has broken down, for only a few of them believe. But perhaps the word 'Israel' should not be understood in that mechanical, humanist way.

Look at the Old Testament. God said to Abraham (9.7), Your descendants shall be counted through Isaac. Abraham had other sons, but Isaac was specially singled out by promise (9.8, 9). It was not the physical descent, but the promise, that mattered. It was the same in the next generation, when Rebecca had twins (9.10–13). And it is always the same. When we are talking about the people of God, we have to deal not with human descent and succession but with God's gracious promise.

But wait a minute, someone will say. This is not fair. What about Ishmael and Esau? Why should they be left out? This complaint is very understandable, and it runs through the rest of the paragraph. In answer, Paul begins by laying the stress where he wants it to lie – on the mercy of God. No man can think that he deserves, or that he can constrain, God's mercy.

It springs from within God himself:

> He hath loved, he hath loved us, because
> he would love.

God's mercy is not the result of man's will or man's effort (9.15, 16); it simply comes from the merciful God.

This, however, is not the whole truth. No one objects when God is merciful. The Old Testament has material to add that is the reverse of this, and it must be fairly faced. God is said to have hardened Pharaoh's heart (9.17, 18; Exodus 4.21). There is no mercy in this, someone will say. But it is wiser not to jump to conclusions. Even Pharaoh plays a positive part in God's purpose. God can and does use him. How could God's power be revealed, and how could his name be spread abroad, if it were not for Pharaoh? God can use the most unlikely persons and circumstances.

Already Paul is working the argument to the point he wants to make (though he will not complete it till he reaches chapter 11); but complaint again breaks out. If God is managing things like this, why does he blame us, who, after all, are only cogs in his machine (9.19)? Here Paul can reply, Who is being unfair now? God is not finding fault; he is being merciful to Gentiles, creatures of his who have been rebellious, and spreading abroad the gospel. How could he have sent it to the Gentiles if the Jews had not spurned it first (9.20–24)? In any case, man is God's creature, and it is not for him to answer back (9.20, 21).

The next few verses (9.25–29), which consist mainly of Old Testament quotations, give us a hint of the line Paul is going to develop later. God knows what he is doing. As far as Israel is concerned, he is working, as usual, not through the whole mass of the people, but through a remnant (9.27, 29). And through this remnant he is working out from Israel towards the world. His purpose is not exclusive, but inclusive; it works, however, in a way that is often mysterious until the goal is reached.

It follows that there are many things we cannot yet understand in the working out of God's purpose; we can, however, clearly see from this chapter how worthless is any claim to belong to God's people which is based on family descent or historical succession. No man belongs to the people of God simply because his father did, or because he belongs to some outwardly continuous organization. At every step, everything depends upon God's merciful purpose, and on a man's own response to it.

13 9.30—10.13
Christ the End of the Law

30 What shall we say, then? That Gentiles who did not pursue righteousness have attained it, that is, righteousness through faith; ³¹ but that Israel who pursued the righteousness which is based on law did not succeed in fulfilling that law. ³² Why? Because they did not pursue it through faith, but as if it were based on works. They have stumbled over the stumbling stone, ³³ as it is written,

'Behold, I am laying in Zion a stone that will make men stumble, a rock that will make them fall;
and he who believes in him will not be put to shame.'

10 Brethren, my heart's desire and prayer to God for them is that they may be saved. ² I bear them witness that they have a zeal for God, but it is not enlightened. ³ For, being ignorant of the righteousness that comes from God, and seeking to establish their own, they did not submit to God's righteousness. ⁴ For Christ is the end of the law, that every one who has faith may be justified.

5 Moses writes that the man who practises the righteousness which is based on the law shall live by it. ⁶ But the righteousness based on faith says, Do not say in your heart, 'Who will ascend into heaven?' (that is, to bring Christ down) ⁷ or 'Who will descend into the abyss?' (that is, to bring Christ up from the dead). ⁸ But what does it say? The word is near you, on your lips and in your heart (that is, the word of faith which we preach); ⁹ because, if you confess with your lips that Jesus is Lord and believe in your heart that God raised him from the dead, you will be saved. ¹⁰ For man believes with his heart and so is justified, and he confesses with his lips and so is saved. ¹¹ The scripture says, 'No one who believes in him will be put to shame.' ¹² For there is no distinction between Jew and Greek; the same Lord is Lord of all and bestows his riches upon all who call upon him. ¹³ For, 'every one who calls upon the name of the Lord will be saved.'

An extraordinary situation has now been disclosed. In the distant past God elected a particular race to be his special people. They were to live by faith in him, to obey his laws and thus to act as his witnesses (Isaiah 43.10) to all other nations. As the greatest of their privileges they were to provide the setting in which God's Son, their Messiah, should be born. Well, he had been born; and his own people, the Jews, had rejected him, though the Gentiles, or some of them, had accepted him. An extraordinary situation indeed, though not a situation out of hand, for God (as Paul shows in the first part of chapter 9) was well able to use it; nevertheless, it was a situation that called for explanation. Why did the Jews reject Christ? Why did the Gentiles believe?

These questions are handled in the last verses of chapter 9, in terms that have become familiar earlier in the letter. Righteousness, not ethical virtue but a right relation with God, is all-important. This the Jews had recognized, but they had supposed that righteousness could be obtained by obedience to law (9.31). They had looked for it in the wrong place; small wonder that they had not found it. The Gentiles at least had the advantage of not looking for righteousness where it was not to be found. They were not interested in law, but, humanly speaking, had accidentally stumbled across righteousness in the gospel (9.30).

Verses 32 and 33 contain a double quotation from Isaiah 8.14 and 28.16, which provides the clue to the situation – to Paul's situation, and to our own. The same object is at once the cause of stumbling, and the centre of faith. This is true about Christ. How could the Jews believe that one so obscurely born, so un-educated, so careless of the details of the law, should be their Messiah? How can people today believe that one who lived nearly two thousand years ago in Palestine, and died on a gibbet, was the Son of God? Yet 'to you who believe he is precious'; in other words, he forces a decision; you must accept or reject him; you cannot be neutral. This is true also about faith. How hard it was for the Jews, and is for us, to believe that God is so easy to approach – that all he asks us to do is to trust him!

The same theme is taken further in the opening verses of chapter 10. Certainly the Jews were zealous in the practice of their religion (10.2) – too zealous perhaps, for they supposed they had to make it work themselves. They were not content to let God act in righteousness, because they were so concerned about their own righteousness (10.3). Verse 4 is very important. Christ is the end of the law, not because he destroys it, but because he fulfils it. All that men had striven vainly to achieve, he himself *is* for everyone (Jew and Gentile) who believes, that is, takes him at his word, and accepts what he gives – righteousness, a right relation with God. Paul goes on to quote Old Testament passages which describe the two attitudes to life that he has in mind, that of human striving, and that of divine grace. Both passages come from 'the Law' (Leviticus 18.5; Deuteronomy 30.12–14); this means that, according to Paul, the law and the gospel, both parts of God's word, do not say completely different things, though some things are said more clearly in the gospel than in the law.

Legal righteousness is a matter of doing (10.5); if you choose that way, you must keep every single commandment before you can talk about life.

What of the righteousness that comes from faith (10.6)? It does not fly up to heaven to bring Christ down, because it knows that God has already (without waiting for men to deserve it) acted in grace and sent his Son (10.6). It does not dive into the deep to bring Christ up from the dead, because it knows that God has already raised him up, beginning the resurrection and establishing the New Age (10.7). What then? The message of faith, the preached gospel (10.8), is the nearest and easiest of all possibilities. God has already put into the heart and mouth of the hearer the appropriate response to the preacher's word. Notice throughout chapter 10 the central importance of preaching in Paul's idea of a gospel ministry.

In verses 9, 10 and 11, Paul carefully explains what the response is, using a very early Christian confession of faith (compare 1 Corinthians 12.3). It is in two parts: (1) Jesus is Lord; (2) God raised him from the dead. The first part is an assertion about Jesus which is at the same time an assertion about Christians. Jesus is the divine king; not merely a teacher, but one who can properly bear the title (Lord) normally given to God himself in the Old Testament. At the same time, those who acknowledge a *lord* confess themselves to be *slaves*, men who owe an absolute and unqualified obedience to a master. The second part of the statement of faith shows that Jesus is not one of the many divine beings believed in by men of old times. In him, especially in his resurrection, we see the eternal and invisible God at work. And in him, we see that God has already set in motion the plan of salvation he has for mankind; the resurrection, the New Age, has begun.

From this it follows at once that those who accept this Lord in obedience and faith will be saved (10.12, 13). If Jesus is the Lord, the 'firstborn from the dead' (Colossians 1.18), this cannot apply only to a fragment of the human race. There is no distinction; 'the invitation is to all'. No one who believes in Christ will have reason to be ashamed; everyone who calls on the Lord in faith will be saved. Paul does not stop here to explain what he means by 'saved'. He has already told us a good deal about it; and there is more to come.

The Way God Works

14 But how are men to call upon him in whom they have not believed? And how are they to believe in him of whom they have never heard? And how are they to hear without a preacher? 15 And how can men preach unless they are sent? As it is written, 'How beautiful are the feet of those who preach good news!' 16 But they have not all obeyed the gospel; for Isaiah says, 'Lord, who has believed what he has heard from us?' 17 So faith comes from what is heard, and what is heard comes by the preaching of Christ.

18 But I ask, have they not heard? Indeed they have; for
'Their voice has gone out to all the earth,
and their words to the ends of the world.'
19 Again I ask, did Israel not understand? First Moses says,
'I will make you jealous of those who are not a nation;
with a foolish nation I will make you angry.'
20 Then Isaiah is so bold as to say,
'I have been found by those who did not seek me;
I have shown myself to those who did not ask for me.'
21 But of Israel he says, 'All day long I have held out my hands to a disobedient and contrary people.'
11 I ask, then, has God rejected his people? By no means! I myself am an Israelite, a descendant of Abraham, a member of the tribe of Benjamin. 2 God has not rejected his people whom he foreknew. Do you not know what the scripture says of Elijah, how he pleads with God against Israel? 3 'Lord, they have killed thy prophets, they have demolished thy altars, and I alone am left, and they seek my life.' 4 But what is God's reply to him? 'I have kept for myself seven thousand men who have not bowed the knee to Baal.' 5 So too at the present time there is a remnant, chosen by grace. 6 But if it is by grace, it is no longer on the basis of works; otherwise grace would no longer be grace.

7 What then? Israel failed to obtain what it sought. The elect obtained it, but the rest were hardened, 8 as it is written,

'God gave them a spirit of stupor,
eyes that should not see and ears that should not hear,
down to this very day.'
9 And David says,
'Let their table become a snare and a trap,
a pitfall and a retribution for them;
10 let their eyes be darkened so that they cannot see,
and bend their backs for ever.'

'Every one who calls upon the name of the Lord will be saved' (10.13). This is splendid – provided that one has heard the Lord's name, and is able to call upon it. This raises a new question, which Paul proceeds to deal with in general terms in verses 14 and 15; later, as we shall see, he comes back to the special problem he is dealing with in chapters 9–11.

'Calling upon the name of the Lord' is far more than knowing how to use the right religious formula; it means trusting the one whose name you invoke, looking to him for salvation. But faith is a big thing, not to be exercised lightly; it can exist only in terms of personal relationship. It is important to notice the correct translation of Paul's words here. He does not say, as the RSV translates the Greek: 'How are they to believe in him of whom they have never heard?' (though this 'of' is still in the NEB). He says: 'How are they to believe in one whom they have never heard?' The implication is clear. In real preaching (which Paul goes on to speak of), we do not simply hear about Christ, we hear Christ himself. Through the unworthy, inadequate, foolish words of a fallible, sinful man, Christ himself speaks. Let preachers remember this, and be humble, and fearless, too. Let congregations remember it, and be thankful. But we must return to the thread of Paul's argument.

You cannot believe in anyone unless you have heard him. How can you hear unless someone proclaims him? The work of preaching is absolutely fundamental in the church; the church

56

cannot live without it. This does not mean that the church cannot live without discourses lasting twenty-five minutes, divided into three parts, and delivered at approximately 11 a.m. and 6.30 p.m. on Sundays! The New Testament itself shows that preaching can take many forms. The most eloquent and formal oration may not be preaching at all; a simple testimony, spoken in one person's ear, may be a true proclamation of the word of God. Preaching in the proper sense takes place, as the Reformers used to say, when and where it pleases God. Men live by it, but they cannot control it. This is implied in Paul's next question: 'How are men to preach unless they are sent?' A man cannot simply stand up, deliver a religious address, and call that preaching. His words become preaching when he is sent by God, when he is (in the full sense of the word) a missionary. We should hope that the church's sending (of ordained ministers and lay preachers) may coincide with God's sending; but the church (like Israel in the Old Testament) may make mistakes about its prophets, and God is completely free to send whom he wills, and to speak through them, whether men are pleased to recognize their 'orders' or not.

Verse 17 sums up the situation so far. Faith comes through hearing, and hearing comes through the word of Christ – the word 'which we preach' (verse 8).

It is valuable beyond measure that Paul should have developed the theme of preaching in this general way, but he was doing it for a particular purpose. From the beginning of chapter 9 he has been struggling with the problem of the unbelief of Israel. What can have gone wrong with God's intention for his people? It is not that God did not send preachers; scripture proves that (verse 15, quoting Isaiah 52.7). It is not that Israel did not hear; scripture proves that (verse 18, quoting Psalm 19.4). The message was not too hard to understand – even Gentiles have understood it: scripture proves that (verses 19, 20, quoting Deuteronomy 32.21; Isaiah 65.1). The failure is in faith; Israel did not believe. Scripture proves that too (verses 16, 21, quoting Isaiah 53.1; 65.2). It is possible to have all the framework and traditions of God's people; without faith these are worthless. And the Gentiles who have faith and nothing else become God's people by their faith alone.

The first paragraph of chapter 11 takes up a new point. The last few verses have spoken once more of Israel's unbelief, and of the Gentiles' faith. Does this mean that God has simply washed his hands of his ancient people (11.1)? That he has made a completely fresh start? No, it cannot mean this. Paul himself, who is writing, is a Jew. And there are more Christian Jews: Peter, James, John, and others Paul could name. It is not true that the whole of Israel has rejected Christ. The existence of this believing group, small as it is, proves that God has not finished with his people. Moreover, there are examples in the past that suggest that it is God's way to work through such groups. Paul quotes only one example (that of Elijah: verses 2–4; see 1 Kings 19.18); any student of the Old Testament could give others, where God seeks and uses a 'remnant' (verse 5) of his people. In verses 5 and 6 Paul points out the significance of this 'seeking'. It means that God is acting in grace. A remnant does not create itself; it comes into being only through God's loving will – deny that, says Paul, and words have simply lost their meaning (verse 6).

So the position reached at this stage is this (verses 7–10). Israel as a whole has rejected God and his word. But, simply of his grace, God has called in Gentiles to receive the gospel, and has also salvaged, out of the wreckage of Israel, a remnant of believers. How God will build on this foundation we shall see in the next section; for the present we may be content to note that, however and whenever he acts, he acts in grace, not because men deserve or secure his favours, but because he loves them, and wills to redeem them.

15 11.11–36

Mercy Triumphant

11 So I ask, have they stumbled so as to fall? By no means! But through their trespass salvation has come to the Gentiles, so as to make Israel jealous. 12 Now if their trespass means riches for the world, and if their failure means riches for the Gentiles, how much more will their full inclusion mean!

13 Now I am speaking to you Gentiles. Inasmuch then as I am an apostle to the Gentiles, I magnify my ministry 14 in order to make my fellow Jews jealous, and thus save some of them. 15 For if their rejection means the reconciliation of the world, what will their acceptance mean but life from the dead? 16 If the dough offered as first fruits is holy, so is the whole lump; and if the root is holy, so are the branches.

17 But if some of the branches were broken off, and you, a wild olive shoot, were grafted in their place to share the richness of the olive tree, 18 do not boast over the branches. If you do boast, remember it is not you that support the root, but the root that supports you. 19 You will say, 'Branches were broken off so that I might be grafted in.' 20 That is true. They were broken off because of their unbelief, but you stand fast only through faith. So do not become proud, but stand in awe. 21 For if God did not spare the natural branches, neither will he spare you. 22 Note then the kindness and the severity of God: severity toward those who have fallen, but God's kindness to you, provided you continue in his kindness; otherwise you too will be cut off. 23 And even the others, if they do not persist in their unbelief, will be grafted in, for God has the power to graft them in again. 24 For if you have been cut from what is by nature a wild olive tree, and grafted, contrary to nature, into a cultivated olive tree, how much more will these natural branches be grafted back into their own olive tree.

25 Lest you be wise in your own conceits, I want you to understand this mystery, brethren: a hardening has come upon part of Israel, until the full number of the Gentiles come in, 26 and so all Israel will be saved; as it is written,

'The Deliverer will come from Zion,
he will banish ungodliness from Jacob';
²⁷ 'and this will be my covenant with them
when I take away their sins.'
²⁸ As regards the gospel they are enemies of God, for your sake; but
as regards election they are beloved for the sake of their forefathers.
²⁹ For the gifts and the call of God are irrevocable. ³⁰ Just as you
were once disobedient to God but now have received mercy because
of their disobedience, ³¹ so they have now been disobedient in order
that by the mercy shown to you they also may receive mercy. ³² For
God has consigned all men to disobedience, that he may have mercy
upon all.

33 O the depth of the riches and wisdom and knowledge of God!
How unsearchable are his judgments and how inscrutable his ways!
³⁴ 'For who has known the mind of the Lord,
or who has been his counsellor?'
³⁵ 'Or who has given a gift to him
that he might be repaid?'
³⁶ For from him and through him and to him are all things. To him
be glory for ever. Amen.

If God is, for the present, left with only a remnant of believing
Jews, and a mere handful of Christian Gentiles, what will he
do for a people? And what will he do about the redemption
of mankind as a whole? These are the questions to which Paul
turns in the remainder of chapter 11. God has not been taken
by surprise; he knows what he will do.

Paul takes up first the question of the Jews (verses 11, 12).
They have stumbled badly; but they have not fallen so as to
be unable ever to rise. In the end, their fall will lead to good,
not evil. To begin with, humanly speaking it is because the
Jews rejected Christ that the Gentiles had a chance of accepting
him. If the Jews had unanimously accepted their own Messiah
there would have been no need for a Gentile mission. But they
rejected him, and the Gentiles have believed. Surely, Paul says,
it will stir up the Jews to envy, when they see Gentiles occupying
the place in God's service they could themselves have had. So
eventually the Jews will be brought up to full strength in the
people of God (see also verses 25, 26, 30, 31). What a blessing

this will be! Their falling away brought the wealth of the gospel to the Gentile world; what will their return mean!

But Paul is writing to Gentiles; he is the apostle of the Gentiles. I make the most of my job, he says (verses 13 and 14), not simply for the Gentiles' sake, but in order, indirectly, to win back the Jews. This is the great objective; verse 15 returns to the theme of verse 12. This leads Paul to an elaborate illustration, which he continues as far as verse 24. I shall divide up what he says in the attempt to make it clear, though indeed the illustration itself is clear enough if the reader will be patient with it.

Paul speaks of an olive tree. He had seen such trees, as the traveller in the eastern Mediterranean can see them today, thickly studded over the countryside. But he is not describing a process that any olive-grower would normally practise; he makes it clear that he is talking of something that is 'contrary to nature' (verse 24). In the ordinary course of things, a farmer would take slips from a cultivated olive tree and graft them into a wild plant, thus eventually producing a new fruit-bearing plant. Paul's process works the other way. He pictures a farmer who starts with a good olive tree, cuts sound branches out of it, and grafts into it slips that he has taken from a wild plant. In due course, however, he returns to the previously excised branches, and grafts them back into the original tree. A strange story indeed; but it proves, not that Paul was a townsman who knew nothing about the country, but that he is arguing from God to nature, not from nature to God. Whatever farmers might do with their olives, this was what God had done with his. His olive was his people, and he had been obliged to cut out branches from it on account of their unbelief (verse 20). Into their places he had grafted fresh branches (verse 17), gathered where he could find them – wild olives, Gentiles. But the story was not to end there. The branches that had been cut out were not discarded; if God could graft in wild branches, much more could he graft in the original shoots of the cultivated olive. In his own good time, the Jews would be gathered in once more.

What have we to learn from this? That God means to have a people; and that he delights in mercy. Who could have blamed him if he had washed his hands of the whole human race? But he did not, and does not; because he is love he means in the end to gather all his family about him. Behold, therefore, God's kindness (verse 22) – and his severity. His kindness never leads him to say, I don't care what they do, I don't care what they believe. God revises his membership-list, and he cuts out dead wood – except that he does not admit that the wood is finally and irrevocably dead. The branches that have been cut out he can graft in again. This, however, is the point at which the illustration breaks down. Branches are branches, and you can put them where you please, but where people are concerned another factor has to be considered – faith. It is for lack of faith that Jewish branches have been cut out, and through faith that Gentile branches have been put in (verse 20). Only continuing faith means continuing inclusion; only continuing unbelief prevents reinstatement (verses 22 and 23). Behind everything is the sheer mercy of God; it is his tree, his people. No one ever gained a place on his own deserts. All man can do, all man must do, is to take God at his word and accept the place he offers.

With verse 25, Paul drops the illustration and speaks in plain prose; I have used what he says in verses 25-32 in the exposition of the olive tree. God knows what he is doing. Paul's missionary work, for all its triumphs, brought him many disappointments. These could not discourage him, because he knew that God was using both failure and success. There is no excuse here for half-hearted or slipshod work, but there is encouragement for the evangelist who has done his best, and fails to see the fruit he longs for. The root of the matter is that God has only one way of dealing with men – in mercy; and to this they must, in one way or another, be brought (verse 32). For Paul this was a matter of Jew and Gentile, but we can make the principle our own. Whatever sort of person I am: gross sinner, busy church worker, untaught child, trained scholar – whatever I am, if I am to know God at all I must know him as the merciful God. He will not despise my wickedness or ignorance; he will not flatter my religion or my learning; he accepts me in mercy.

No wonder Paul breaks out into the doxology of the concluding verses. 'O the depth of the riches and wisdom and knowledge of God!' (verse 33). All things begin from him, all things are directed by him, all things end in him (verse 36). To God, this God, who has loved us and loosed us from our sins, be glory for ever. The remainder of the epistle is a comment on this shout of praise.

16

Life in the Church

1 I appeal to you therefore, brethren, by the mercies of God, to present your bodies as a living sacrifice, holy and acceptable to God, which is your spiritual worship. ²Do not be conformed to this world but be transformed by the renewal of your mind, that you may prove what is the will of God, what is good and acceptable and perfect.

3 For by the grace given to me I bid every one among you not to think of himself more highly than he ought to think, but to think with sober judgment, each according to the measure of faith which God has assigned him. ⁴For as in one body we have many members, and all the members do not have the same function, ⁵so we, though many, are one body in Christ, and individually members one of another. ⁶Having gifts that differ according to the grace given to us, let us use them; if prophecy, in proportion to our faith; ⁷if service, in our serving; he who teaches, in his teaching; ⁸he who exhorts, in his exhortation; he who contributes, in liberality; he who gives aid, with zeal; he who does acts of mercy, with cheerfulness.

9 Let love be genuine; hate what is evil, hold fast to what is good; ¹⁰love one another with brotherly affection; outdo one another in showing honour. ¹¹Never flag in zeal, be aglow with the Spirit, serve the Lord. ¹²Rejoice in your hope, be patient in tribulation, be constant in prayer. ¹³ Contribute to the needs of the saints, practise hospitality.

14 Bless those who persecute you; bless and do not curse them. ¹⁵Rejoice with those who rejoice, weep with those who weep. ¹⁶Live in harmony with one another; do not be haughty, but associate with the lowly; never be conceited. ¹⁷Repay no one evil for evil, but take thought for what is noble in the sight of all. ¹⁸If possible, so far as it depends upon you, live peaceably with all. ¹⁹Beloved, never avenge yourselves, but leave it to the wrath of God; for it is written, 'Vengeance is mine, I will repay, says the Lord.' ²⁰No, 'if your enemy is hungry, feed him; if he is thirsty, give him drink; for by so doing you will heap burning coals upon his head.' ²¹Do not be overcome by evil but overcome evil with good.

'To God be the glory!' That was the point at which we left Paul at the end of chapter 11. It is also the point at which many people cease their study of the epistle. We have, they think, had 'all the theology' and 'all the gospel'. We have read of the universal sinfulness of mankind, and of the universal grace of God; of his infinite love in sending his Son to die for our sins, and of the free justification by faith alone which, in his mercy, he offers. We have read of the power of the Spirit of God to bring life out of death; of predestination, and God's eternal purpose for his creatures. But there are five chapters before us, and though some of them are bound up with the special situation of Paul and of the Roman church, they are all more or less directly applicable to ourselves and to leave them out upsets the balance, and destroys a large part of the content, of Paul's message.

In fact, chapter 12 is very closely joined to chapters 1–11. Note the 'therefore' (12.1): what follows is a logical consequence of what goes before. This is expanded in 'by the mercies of God' – for what are chapters 1–11 about if they are not about God's mercy? Because God is what he is, and has done what he has done, certain things follow; or rather, ought to follow. There is no compulsion; Paul can only make an appeal to his readers: I beseech you.

It is important here for a moment to look further ahead than we can go in the present exposition. There is a quantity of exhortation in chapters 12 and 13, and it is set in a framework consisting of 12.1, 2 and 13.11–14. The latter passage should be read now; I shall return to it in due course. For the present we must confine our attention to 12.1, 2. To understand these verses we must remember that Paul, like most of his fellow-Jews, thought of time as split up into two parts: this age, and the age to come. 'This age' was the time of revolt against God, in which sin, and consequently suffering and death, prevailed. 'The age to come' was the time when God would bring all things into subjection to himself, redeem his people, and put an end to evil. These ideas were familiar to Paul, but when he became a Christian he was obliged to see them in a new light. Sin and death were still with him; the glory of the coming kingdom of God was still in the future. But Jesus, God's Messiah, had come; and though he had died, he had risen from the dead. This meant that the old age was on the way out; the new age had dawned.

This explains verse 2. It is easy to take the shape of this age; it is round about us, pressing on every side. It is very natural that our thinking and living should be dictated by our neighbours – very natural, and, if we are Christians, quite wrong. If we really believe in Jesus as God's Messiah, we must let our minds be renewed, and live by a new set of values, determined by God's perfect will. The way into this renewal is the true, spiritual worship of God, which does not require conventional gifts, or any outward act or word at all, but the offering in sacrifice of our bodies (verse 1) – not simply the spiritual or intellectual side of life, but our bodies, the whole equipment God has given to us as a means of expressing ourselves.

The rest of the chapter works out the practical application of this offering of our bodies to God. It requires not so much to be explained as to be carried out. Most of the chapter, and especially verses 3–8, deals with the relation of Christians to one another. We have met earlier in the epistle the important phrase 'in Christ' (for example 3.24; 6.23; 8.1). Every Christian is in Christ, but not simply as an individual. Christians are in Christ as a body, and a body is marked by both unity and diversity. Its parts are different from one another but they all work together (verse 4). It is the same with Christians. All have some gift from God, but the gifts differ (verse 6). For this reason Christians should neither envy nor despise one another; each one should use his gift to the full for the benefit of the community as a whole.

The gifts Paul refers to in verses 6–8 are of three kinds, which it is important to note, because between them they sum up the services that the church needs. (1) There are gifts expressed through speech – prophecy, teaching, exhorting. The church lives by the word of God, and these gifts (which together we might call preaching) are essential to its life. (2) There are gifts expressed in practical service – ministry, giving, showing mercy (to use the RV translations). A church that does not back up its spoken witness with this acted witness of love is not the church of Christ. (3) There is the gift of presiding, or taking the lead (RV's 'he that ruleth' is much too strong). There are Christians who are able to guide the community as a whole, and take some responsibility for the welfare of others. All these three gifts we expect today to see exercised by ministers, but Paul thinks of them as distributed, and exercised, throughout the community. Every Christian may well bear witness to his faith in word and deed, and feel an active responsibility for his brother.

The rest of the chapter underlines especially the importance of mutual love (verses 9, 10, 13, 15), and of love even for enemies (verses 14, 17, 19–21). Paul is very close to his master's teaching here, though we cannot point to any direct quotation from the words of Jesus. Humility also is an outstanding Christian virtue (verses 3, 10, 16); and Christians must always seek peace (verses 18–21), though Paul recognizes that peace may sometimes be broken through others' fault. There are limits to the peacefulness of those whose duty it is to bear witness to the truth, and to care for their brethren. Even so, it is never right for Christians to allow themselves to be overmastered by such an evil as hatred; if they are more than conquerors (8.37) they must see their victory issue in the supremacy of love and goodness.

17

13.1–14

Perfect Love

1 Let every person be subject to the governing authorities. For there is no authority except from God, and those that exist have been instituted by God. ²Therefore he who resists the authorities resists what God has appointed, and those who resist will incur judgment. ³For rulers are not a terror to good conduct, but to bad. Would you have no fear of him who is in authority? Then do what is good, and you will receive his approval, ⁴for he is God's servant for your good. But if you do wrong, be afraid, for he does not bear the sword in vain; he is the servant of God to execute his wrath on the wrong-doer. ⁵Therefore one must be subject, not only to avoid God's wrath but also for the sake of conscience. ⁶For the same reason you also pay taxes, for the authorities are ministers of God, attending to this very thing. ⁷Pay all of them their dues, taxes to whom taxes are due, revenue to whom revenue is due, respect to whom respect is due, honour to whom honour is due.

8 Owe no one anything, except to love one another; for he who loves his neighbour has fulfilled the law. ⁹The commandments, 'You shall not commit adultery, You shall not kill, You shall not steal, You shall not covet', and any other commandment, are summed up in this sentence, 'You shall love your neighbour as yourself.' ¹⁰Love does no wrong to a neighbour; therefore love is the fulfilling of the law.

11 Besides this you know what hour it is, how it is full time now for you to wake from sleep. For salvation is nearer to us now than when we first believed; ¹²the night is far gone, the day is at hand. Let us then cast off the works of darkness and put on the armour of light; ¹³let us conduct ourselves becomingly as in the day, not in revelling and drunkenness, not in debauchery and licentiousness, not in quarrelling and jealousy. ¹⁴But put on the Lord Jesus Christ, and make no provision for the flesh, to gratify its desires.

There is no break between chapter 12 and chapter 13. In chapter 12, after stating the fundamental principle in verses 1 and 2,

Paul goes on to show how the Christian's life of gratitude to God must be worked out in a number of situations. These belong to the life of the Christian within the Christian community, which forms one body in Christ. Here men must exercise their varying gifts for the good of all; here they must be humble and peaceable. There is no need to say that this is of the highest importance. It does not, however, make up the whole life of the Christian, who is a member not only of the church but also of society at large. It is not his Christian duty to withdraw from society, but to live in it a life of Christian responsibility. This is the theme of 13.1–7.

In verse 1, the 'governing authorities' to which Paul refers are to be understood as the authorities governing the Roman Empire, the political framework within which all Paul's work was carried out. There are some who think that the phrase includes also the spiritual, or demonic forces, behind the political authorities, but this view is not so probable. People have often wondered how Paul could write, during the reign of Nero, that the supreme authorities – the Emperor himself – had been appointed by God. There are several things to say about this, some historical, some exegetical and theological.

(1) Paul was writing about AD 55. Nero reigned from 54 to 68, and it is a well-known fact that the first five years of his reign were years of good government; it was only later that he became a notoriously evil figure.

(2) Even in his later years, his cruelty was felt mainly in the city of Rome itself; the provinces (so far the scene of Paul's labours) continued to be well governed.

(3) God's appointment of the political authorities is part of his providence; he provides them as he provides the sunshine and rain, in order that the world may continue. This is not to say that he approves of everything they do. The world as a whole is a world that has gone wrong (compare 8.20, 21) and in it God's rain and sun do apparent harm as well as good. The same is true of rulers.

(4) The word which RSV translates 'be subject to' must be

69

carefully understood. When it is used at Colossians 3.18, it does not mean (to take an extreme example) that a woman must commit murder if her husband tells her to do so. It means that God has made arrangements for the proper working of the family, and that his creatures should observe them. It is so here. God wills government, not anarchy; but this does not mean (and Paul did not take it to mean) that Christians must obey every wicked command of godless men. In particular, when a government rebels against God who appointed it, it may become a Christian duty to rebel against the government – in the interests of good government.

The rest of the paragraph now becomes clear. The state is God's servant (verse 4) both negatively and positively (verse 3). Its judgment anticipates God's wrath at the last judgment (verse 4); the state's moral authority thus helps to prevent moral collapse. The state has a claim, not merely on the respect but on the support of Christians (verse 6). Paul does not contemplate a situation in which there was any prospect of Christians actually taking a personal share in the work of government; one has only to think of the minute and socially insignificant number of Christians in the first century to see why. But he does urge them to pay their taxes, and thus make what contribution they can. In a world of far larger opportunities for Christian social service we ought to make a correspondingly larger contribution. Neither irresponsibility nor disrespect (verse 7) is a Christian virtue; and if there are times when conscience compels a Christian to dissent from the social framework in which he lives this is in order that political life may be brought more completely into obedience to God.

In verses 8–10, Paul returns to the theme of love, emphasizing it here as the all-inclusive command which carries with it everything else. When Wesley described the Christian ideal as 'perfect love' he was following Paul – and for that matter John, and Jesus himself. In the use he makes of Leviticus 19.18, Paul comes very near to quoting Jesus (see Mark 12.31), but he does not claim his authority. Perhaps he was afraid of turning Jesus into but another rabbi, whose teaching on this or that subject might be quoted and discussed. For Paul, the really important thing about Jesus was not what he said, but what he was and what he did. It is important to notice Paul's use of the Old Testament. The supreme command, which God lays upon Christians (and upon all men), is not a new discovery, but was already written in the Old Testament. The new thing is not a fresh ethical precept, but the fact that love can no longer be misunderstood in terms of desire (compare 7.7, 8). The love that fulfils the law is plainly to be seen in Jesus Christ. 'God shows his love for us in that while we were yet sinners Christ died for us' (5.8). 'He loved me, and gave himself for me' (Galatians 2.20).

In dealing with chapter 12, I pointed out that the great block of moral teaching contained in chapters 12 and 13 is enclosed in a framework consisting of 12.1, 2 and 13.11–14. We saw then that Paul was able, in Christ's name, to make his claim upon Christians because the old age was drawing to its close and the new age had dawned. It is, however, true that the old age is still with us, and the new age has not come. But it is near. The night is far spent; the day is at hand (verse 12). In this fact Paul sees a special reason (verse 11) for ending the old way of life, and embarking on the new life in Christ (verses 12–14).

In terms of clock and calendar the new day was not as near as Paul himself perhaps thought; but what he says is true. We who live 'after Christ' are living in the last chapter of the world's history, however long the chapter may turn out to be, and we must live with God's future in mind. That is why the words of verses 13 and 14 could become the occasion of Augustine's conversion in AD 386, and why Wesley could say of them (in his *Notes on the New Testament*), 'Herein is contained the whole of our salvation.'

How to Deal with a Problem

1 As for the man who is weak in faith, welcome him, but not for disputes over opinions. ²One believes he may eat anything, while the weak man eats only vegetables. ³Let not him who eats despise him who abstains, and let not him who abstains pass judgment on him who eats; for God has welcomed him. ⁴Who are you to pass judgment on the servant of another? It is before his own master that he stands or falls. And he will be upheld, for the Master is able to make him stand.

5 One man esteems one day as better than another, while another man esteems all days alike. Let every one be fully convinced in his own mind. ⁶He who observes the day, observes it in honour of the Lord. He also who eats, eats in honour of the Lord, since he gives thanks to God; while he who abstains, abstains in honour of the Lord and gives thanks to God. ⁷None of us lives to himself, and none of us dies to himself. ⁸If we live, we live to the Lord, and if we die, we die to the Lord; so then, whether we live or whether we die, we are the Lord's. ⁹For to this end Christ died and lived again, that he might be Lord both of the dead and of the living.

10 Why do you pass judgment on your brother? Or you, why do you despise your brother? For we shall all stand before the judgment seat of God; ¹¹for it is written,

'As I live, says the Lord, every knee shall bow to me,
and every tongue shall give praise to God.'

¹²So each of us shall give account of himself to God.

13 Then let us no more pass judgment on one another, but rather decide never to put a stumbling block or hindrance in the way of a brother. ¹⁴I know and am persuaded in the Lord Jesus that nothing is unclean in itself; but it is unclean for any one who thinks it unclean. ¹⁵If your brother is being injured by what you eat, you are no longer walking in love. Do not let what you eat cause the ruin of one for whom Christ died. ¹⁶So do not let your good be spoken of as evil. ¹⁷For the kingdom of God is not food and drink but righteousness and peace and joy in the Holy Spirit; ¹⁸he who thus serves Christ

is acceptable to God and approved by men. ¹⁹Let us then pursue what makes for peace and for mutual upbuilding. ²⁰Do not, for the sake of food, destroy the work of God. Everything is indeed clean, but it is wrong for any one to make others fall by what he eats; ²¹it is right not to eat meat or drink wine or do anything that makes your brother stumble. ²²The faith that you have, keep between yourself and God; happy is he who has no reason to judge himself for what he approves. ²³But he who has doubts is condemned, if he eats, because he does not act from faith; for whatever does not proceed from faith is sin.

One reason why Romans is specially important for us to study is the fact that Paul had never been to Rome. When he writes, for example, to Corinth, everything he says is applied to a particular situation. This does not make it unimportant, but it means that before we can use it we have to detach it from the Corinthian situation and fit it into our own. In Romans we can, for the most part, leave out the process of 'detaching', and read the epistle immediately in our own situation. With chapter 14, however, we come to a state of affairs which Paul must have heard of as prevailing in the Roman church of his day; and our first task is to describe the situation.

It seems that there were two groups of Christians, one called (presumably by the others) 'weak' (14.1), the other described (presumably by themselves) as 'strong' (15.1). The weak ate vegetables only, abstaining from meat (14.2), drank no wine (verse 21), and observed special days, probably sabbaths and other religious seasons (verse 5). The strong observed none of these practices, treating all foods and drinks, and all days, alike (verses 2, 5). The weak, who laid great store by their observances, were censorious, and passed judgment on the strong, who seemed to them careless and indifferent (verses 3, 4, 10, 13). The strong, who did not feel bound by religious rules, despised those who kept them (verses 3, 10). Such a situation, in which the strict pass judgment on those whom they think lax, and the free despise those whom they think rigid, is not unfamiliar.

The first point to grasp is that Paul counts himself one of the 'strong' (15.1). He recognizes that in principle they are right. It ought to be made clear that the views Paul is dealing with here are purely religious views. The conviction that alcohol (in wine or other drinks) is harmful to the body, causes accidents and other suffering, and is an unwarrantable expense, is not under discussion. The weak Christians in Rome did not abstain from wine for these reasons, but because they thought that by doing so a man could win a higher standing with God. If they were right in thinking this, then the whole of Romans is wrong, for in it Paul teaches repeatedly that we cannot stand before God on the basis of religious works, but only by grace and through faith. He duly follows this principle to its conclusion – a conclusion in which Jesus (Mark 7.17–23) had anticipated him. Nothing is unclean in itself (verse 14): Everything is clean (verse 20).

What is the inference? That the strong have won, and that the weak are defeated, and must either give in or get out of the church? Not at all. I have just quoted two half-verses. Verse 14 continues: Only to a man who reckons anything to be unclean, to him it is unclean. Verse 20 continues: But they work harm to the man who eats them so as to cause offence. The position is not so simple as it seems. It is never sufficient for me to consider whether what I do is in principle right; I must also consider my fellow-Christian, and the effect of my actions on him.

First, I must remember that he is a Christian. I may think he takes dangerous liberties, or that he is an old stick-in-the-mud; and I may be right. But he is a Christian, and this depends not on what I think of him, but on what Christ thinks of him. God has welcomed him, and the Lord has power to make him stand (verses 3, 4). It may still be true that he is a deluded Christian, whom I should try to win to a better mind; but I must not begin by denying that he is a Christian.

Because we are both Christians, he and I, the things we do (or do not do), we do for Christ. If I visit my neighbour and

74

find him sitting down to an ascetic meal that would not suit me, or to a table loaded with food and wine that I should condemn as wanton luxury, I know nevertheless that he has said grace over his food; he has given God thanks (verse 6), and in this, as in everything else a Christian does in life or death, he is the Lord's (verses 7–9). He and I will both stand before God's judgment-seat, and I am not the judge (verse 10).

Again, I must remember that my brother has a conscience. It is his conscience (even though it be misguided) that tells him to keep his religious rules. If I flout his conscience, he will be hurt. This may happen in three ways. (1) He may simply be grieved (verse 15). If this happens, it is no good my saying that he is a foolish man; I have hurt him, and this means that I am disobeying God's command that I should love him (13.8–10). (2) I may split the church. This seems to be meant in verse 20, for the 'work of God', which must not be overthrown, is probably not simply God's work in the individual believer but his work in calling together his people. We should seek to build up (verse 19) the church, not to split it up and cast it down. (3) The greatest, because the most subtle, danger is that my brother, seeing my example, may be encouraged to do what I do, even though his conscience forbids him, and he still has doubts (verse 23). It is not sin for me to do what my conscience approves, but if another follows my example, perhaps because he fears my scorn, then he sins, and I sin because I have made him sin.

This discussion of a special Roman problem not only shows Paul's amazing magnanimity, sympathy, and pastoral wisdom; it leads us to truths with important applications for ourselves. There is no room to work these out here, and it is better that the reader should work them out for himself; but before we leave chapter 14, two verses must be underlined.

Verse 23: Whatever does not proceed from faith is sin. The only right relation with God is that of faith, the faith that recognizes that no amount of keeping the rules will justify us, and leaves the responsibility where it belongs, with God. Anything beyond this, any attempt to rely on or to square our own conscience, is sin, because it does not give God *all* the glory. Verse 17 puts the same truth positively. Food laws, whether we keep them or despise them, do not bring us into the kingdom. That is the work of the Spirit, and the fruit he gives (compare Galatians 5.22, 23) is righteousness, peace and joy.

19 $^{15.1-33}$

An Evangelist and his Plans

1 We who are strong ought to bear with the failings of the weak, and not to please ourselves; ²let each of us please his neighbour for his good, to edify him. ³For Christ did not please himself; but, as it is written, 'The reproaches of those who reproached thee fell on me.' ⁴For whatever was written in former days was written for our instruction, that by steadfastness and by the encouragement of the scriptures we might have hope. ⁵May the God of steadfastness and encouragement grant you to live in such harmony with one another, in accord with Christ Jesus, ⁶that together you may with one voice glorify the God and Father of our Lord Jesus Christ.

7 Welcome one another, therefore, as Christ has welcomed you, for the glory of God. ⁸For I tell you that Christ became a servant to the circumcised to show God's truthfulness, in order to confirm the promises given to the patriarchs, ⁹and in order that the Gentiles might glorify God for his mercy. As it is written,

'Therefore I will praise thee among the Gentiles,
  and sing to thy name';
¹⁰and again it is said,
'Rejoice, O Gentiles, with his people';
¹¹and again,
'Praise the Lord, all Gentiles,
  and let all the peoples praise him';
¹²and further Isaiah says,
'The root of Jesse shall come,
  he who rises to rule the Gentiles;
  in him shall the Gentiles hope.'
¹³May the God of hope fill you with all joy and peace in believing, so that by the power of the Holy Spirit you may abound in hope.

14 I myself am satisfied about you, my brethren, that you yourselves are full of goodness, filled with all knowledge, and able to instruct one another. ¹⁵But on some points I have written to you very boldly

by way of reminder, because of the grace given me by God ¹⁶to be a minister of Christ Jesus to the Gentiles in the priestly service of the gospel of God, so that the offering of the Gentiles may be acceptable, sanctified by the Holy Spirit. ¹⁷In Christ Jesus, then, I have reason to be proud of my work for God. ¹⁸For I will not venture to speak of anything except what Christ has wrought through me to win obedience from the Gentiles, by word and deed, ¹⁹by the power of signs and wonders, by the power of the Holy Spirit, so that from Jerusalem and as far round as Illyricum I have fully preached the gospel of Christ, ²⁰ thus making it my ambition to preach the gospel, not where Christ has already been named, lest I build on another man's foundation, ²¹but as it is written,

'They shall see who have never been told of him,
and they shall understand who have never heard of him.'

22 This is the reason why I have so often been hindered from coming to you.²³But now, since I no longer have any room for work in these regions, and since I have longed for many years to come to you, ²⁴I hope to see you in passing as I go to Spain, and to be sped on my journey there by you, once I have enjoyed your company for a little. ²⁵At present, however, I am going to Jerusalem with aid for the saints. ²⁶For Macedonia and Achaia have been pleased to make some contribution for the poor among the saints at Jerusalem; ²⁷they were pleased to do it, and indeed they are in debt to them, for if the Gentiles have come to share in their spiritual blessings, they ought also to be of service to them in material blessings. ²⁸When therefore I have completed this, and have delivered to them what has been raised, I shall go on by way of you to Spain; ²⁹and I know that when I come to you I shall come in the fullness of the blessing of Christ.

30 I appeal to you, brethren, by our Lord Jesus Christ and by the love of the Spirit, to strive together with me in your prayers to God on my behalf, ³¹that I may be delivered from the unbelievers in Judea, and that my service for Jerusalem may be acceptable to the saints, ³²so that by God's will I may come to you with joy and be refreshed in your company. ³³The God of peace be with you all. Amen.

This chapter falls into two clearly divided parts. The first, verses 1–13, is the continuation of chapter 14, in which Paul dealt with the problem of the 'strong' and the 'weak', the free and the scrupulous, Christians in Rome. It was essential, he said, that each should consider not only himself and his own conscience, but also his brother and his brother's conscience. To clinch the argument he now turns to the example of Christ.

The first two verses take up what Paul has already said. He himself is one of the 'strong', only it is the duty of people like him not to mock at the 'weak' but to bear their burdens, having a view to the good of all and the building up of the church. It is not for them to please themselves; this is something Christ never did (verse 3). It is no doubt true that in saying this Paul had in mind the record of the earthly life of Jesus – his readiness to heal disease, and to serve his fellow-men, even to the extent of giving his life for them. Paul does not, however, illustrate his point by using stories about Jesus, but by quoting the Old Testament (Psalm 69.9). This may seem to us less effective; it is in fact even more meaningful, for in fulfilling scripture Jesus was not simply showing what he himself was like, but revealing the nature of God, and what God had always intended as the right way for men to live.

Paul develops this point about scripture in the next verse (4): the Old Testament is not out of date, but was written for the instruction of Christians, and to give them hope – hope, because it shows that what they have learnt of Christ is the eternal will of God, and therefore must prevail in the end. In verses 5 and 6 Paul sums up so far in a prayer that his readers may be united in a common mind and in the praise of God. This prayer, however, needs to be brought more explicitly into the situation at Rome. 'Welcome one another, as Christ has welcomed you' (verse 7). Christ did not wait for you to become perfectly good, religious, and orthodox before he accepted you; he received you, a guilty sinner, as soon as you looked to him. He did the same for your brother. And there is no reason why you should not do as much for one another. The exact meaning of verse 8 is much disputed. Probably (but not certainly) the point is: I am telling you 'strong' Christians to put up with the religious odd-ness of the 'weak', and this is precisely what Christ did, for he made himself the servant of the oddest of all religious people –

79

the Jews, here appropriately described as 'the circumcision'. He did this in order to confirm God's promises to their fathers, but in such a way that the Gentiles might in the end be included by God's mercy among his people (compare chapter 11). A final prayer, in verse 13, gives another picture of the breadth and depth of the Christian life.

The second part of the chapter begins at verse 14, and here the letter begins to move to its close.

We are familiar with the Epistle to the Romans, because it is part of the Bible; we do not often consider how strange it is that it should ever have been written. It was against Paul's principles to interfere in churches that he had not founded (15.20), and he feels it necessary to explain why he should make an exception to his rule. It was not that the Romans did not know the gospel, or that they needed an extra apostle to manage their affairs for them. They could deal with their own problems (verse 14). Paul does not venture to take the position of a bishop, or archbishop; he is an evangelist (verses 15, 16). He knows well, however, that the responsibilities of an evangelist do not cease at the moment of conversion. He reminds his converts (of what they already know), and so ministers to them that they may be a holy offering to God.

All this is true, but it does not explain why Paul should write to Rome, for the Roman Christians were not his converts. The fact is that he was planning a new development in his apostolic work for the Gentiles. Constantly pressing on, he had covered the north-eastern quarter of the Mediterranean world (Jerusalem to Illyricum – look at a map). Rome had been evangelized by others, and the next stage was Spain. It is interesting that Paul shows no concern for the African coast; perhaps he knew that others were at work there. If, however, he was to get to Spain he needed a new base; Antioch and even Ephesus were too remote. What could the new base be but Rome (verses 24, 28)? Hence the letter.

There was another duty to see to first. For some years Paul had been hard at work on a collection for the relief of poor

Christians in Jerusalem, in which he saw not only an act of practical Christian love but a means of cementing the unity of the original Jewish church with his own Gentile churches. He knew that this task would not be easy; there would be danger from unbelieving Jews, and he could not be certain what reception he would get from the Jewish Christians (verse 31). Part of what happened we can read in Acts. Paul did eventually reach Rome, not as a free man ready to move on to Spain, but as a Roman prisoner.

With a clear understanding of the perils, and with a fervent desire to take with him wherever he went the fullness of the blessing of Christ (verse 29), Paul has a last word for his readers. He urges them to join him in prayer; not merely to pray, but to wrestle in prayer. They were not apostles; God did not wish them to be apostles. But they could share in the church's apostolic mission by praying for the missionaries. So can we. And it is evident that by prayer Paul does not mean two or three perfunctory minutes, morning and night (though that is better than nothing), but a tremendous, Spirit-filled activity. How much the apostles of the first century, and of the twentieth, depend on this, perhaps even they do not fully know; but God does.

Products of the Gospel

1 I commend to you our sister Phoebe, a deaconess of the church at Cenchreae, ²that you may receive her in the Lord as befits the saints, and help her in whatever she may require from you, for she has been a helper of many and of myself as well.

3 Greet Prisca and Aquila, my fellow workers in Christ Jesus,⁴ who risked their necks for my life, to whom not only I but also all the churches of the Gentiles give thanks; ⁵greet also the church in their house. Greet my beloved Epaenetus, who was the first convert in Asia for Christ. ⁶Greet Mary, who has worked hard among you. ⁷Greet Andronicus and Junias, my kinsmen and my fellow prisoners; they are men of note among the apostles, and they were in Christ before me. ⁸Greet Ampliatus, my beloved in the Lord. ⁹Greet Urbanus, our fellow worker in Christ, and my beloved Stachys. ¹⁰Greet Apelles, who is approved in Christ. Greet those who belong to the family of Aristobulus. ¹¹Greet my kinsman Herodion. Greet those in the Lord who belong to the family of Narcissus. ¹²Greet those workers in the Lord, Tryphaena and Tryphosa. Greet the beloved Persis, who has worked hard in the Lord. ¹³Greet Rufus, eminent in the Lord, also his mother and mine. ¹⁴Greet Asyncritus, Phlegon, Hermes, Patrobas, Hermas, and the brethren who are with them. ¹⁵Greet Philologus, Julia, Nereus and his sister, and Olympas, and all the saints who are with them. ¹⁶Greet one another with a holy kiss. All the churches of Christ greet you.

17 I appeal to you, brethren, to take note of those who create dissensions and difficulties, in opposition to the doctrine which you have been taught; avoid them. ¹⁸For such persons do not serve our Lord Christ, but their own appetites, and by fair and flattering words they deceive the hearts of the simple-minded. ¹⁹For while your obedience is known to all, so that I rejoice over you, I would have you wise as to what is good and guileless as to what is evil; ²⁰then the God of peace will soon crush Satan under your feet. The grace of our Lord Jesus Christ be with you.

21 Timothy, my fellow worker, greets you; so do Lucius and Jason and Sosipater, my kinsmen.

22 I Tertius, the writer of this letter, greet you in the Lord.

23 Gaius, who is host to me and to the whole church, greets you. Erastus, the city treasurer, and our brother Quartus, greet you.

25 Now to him who is able to strengthen you according to my gospel and the preaching of Jesus Christ, according to the revelation of the mystery which was kept secret for long ages [26] but is now disclosed and through the prophetic writings is made known to all nations, according to the command of the eternal God, to bring about the obedience of faith – [27] to the only wise God be glory for evermore through Jesus Christ! Amen.

The letter is at an end. Paul has said what he wants to say, and comes finally to the personal messages he has to send. How he knew by name so many people in a church he had not visited is something of a mystery, and there are some who think that chapter 16, though written by Paul, was originally sent by him not to Rome but to Ephesus, where he had lived for some time and had many friends. This may be true; I prefer to think that he gathered up all the personal contacts he could find in order to make the links he was evidently looking for in chapter 15. We must not underestimate the amount of travelling that went on in Paul's day.

This guessing is not very important. What we may find in chapter 16 is a series of thumbnail sketches of first century Christians. As we read through the greater part of Romans we may well find ourselves saying: Here is the gospel, as Paul understood it; what sort of people did it make? The answer is before us.

Paul begins (verses 1, 2) with a recommendation of Phoebe, who was evidently on her travels, and would find herself in a strange place without friends – or would have done so but for the church. The new faith provided a universal fellowship. Phoebe was some sort of minister in the church at Cenchreae (near Corinth); it is pointless to ask exactly what sort, since in Paul's time there were few rigid dividing lines (perhaps we have too many). She, like the rest, did the service to which God called her, and this was gratefully recognized. Prisca and

83

Aquila were old friends, and we read of them in Acts (Prisca is Priscilla there), though unfortunately Acts tells us nothing of the occasion when they risked their lives for Paul's. All the churches had reason to be grateful to them; and there was a church that met in their house. The first Christian assemblies were 'cottage meetings', and there is much to be said for them. Small groups meeting outside church premises might be one of the spearheads of evangelism today.

Epaenetus (verse 5) was the first convert in the Roman province of Asia. How easy it is to say that! And what a tremendous thing it was, when for the first time, in a vast area and a huge population, a man had the grace and courage to say: 'Jesus is Lord!' Of Mary (verse 6), and many others, all we know is that they joined in Christian work: preaching the gospel, caring for the needy, building up the fellowship. We should dearly like to know more of what they did, but there is no means of finding out. What matters is that they did their service, and the Lord knew what they did, and blessed it. The same applies to us. Most of our Christian service goes unrecorded, but that does not matter so long as it is service the Lord can use.

Andronicus and Junias (verse 7) had been in prison with Paul (or, at least, like Paul). They, too, were apostles – a reminder that this word does not apply exclusively to Paul and the Twelve. Rufus (verse 13) was an outstanding Christian – one of the 'picked troops', as it were, for the word 'chosen' (RV), though it can be applied to all Christians, who are God's elect (for example, 8.33), must have a special sense here – hence RSV's 'eminent'.

The greetings come from Paul, but they come from all the churches, too (verse 16). No one was in as good a position as Paul to know the mind of all the churches, and to represent them. There are more personal greetings in verses 21–23: from Timothy, about whom we know a good deal, and from others, of whom we know next to nothing. A mixed company, these first century Christians, just as we are; but they all have their place in Christ, and in his church. He is big enough to deal with them all, with the outstanding, like Rufus, and with the ordinary and unknown. There is no suggestion of any hierarchy among them, except the hierarchy of service. Paul has learnt from his Lord: Whoever would become great among you shall be your servant, and whoever would be first among you shall be slave of all (Mark 10.43, 44). They are a family, of brothers, sisters, and mothers (verse 13); not an institution.

I have jumped over verses 17–20, where Paul remembers once more the danger of division in the church. He must give a final warning against the trouble-makers. He does not blame them for rebelling against an organization – we have just seen that there was very little organization for them to rebel against; he does blame them for deserting the sound teaching that had been given them (verse 17). They do this because they 'serve their own appetites' (verse 18). This probably does not mean that they are greedy, but that they want to introduce Jewish food-laws, and thus corrupt the gospel. We hear more of such men in other letters. Paul's readers must be content to go in the way of simple faith and obedience, and to fight the good fight. Victory is sure, because the battle is God's; and it will not be long delayed (verse 20).

Verses 25–27 bring the letter to a close, by pointing once more to Jesus Christ, the one in whom God's eternal purposes are fulfilled and made known, the one to whom all nations must look in faith for salvation, giving glory to God through him. If we had Paul's insight, we should see the whole of the Epistle to the Romans, and the whole of Christian life and doctrine, in these two points.

> Look unto him, ye nations; own
>   Your God, ye fallen race;
> Look, and be saved through faith alone,
>   Be justified by grace.

To God be the glory! Great things he hath done.